ACPL ITEM
DISCARDED

ALLEN COUNTY PUBLIC LIBRARY

P9-EEN-479

PARENT-TEACHER COLLECTION

Energy
and Change

Elementary Science Activity Series

High/Scope Elementary Curriculum Materials

Elementary Curriculum Guides

Foundations in Elementary Education: Movement
Foundations in Elementary Education: Music
Foundations in Elementary Education: Overview
Language & Literacy
Learning Environment
Mathematics
Science

Elementary Curriculum Videotapes

Active Learning
Classroom Environment
Language & Literacy
Mathematics

Related Movement and Music Materials

Teaching Movement & Dance: A Sequential Approach to Rhythmic Movement,
　　Third Edition
Round the Circle: Key Experiences in Movement for Children
Movement Plus Music: Activities for Children Ages 3 to 7, Second Edition
Movement Plus Rhymes, Songs, & Singing Games
Movement in Steady Beat
Rhythmically Moving 1–9 (records, cassettes, CDs)
Changing Directions 1–6 (records, cassettes, CDs)
Foundations in Elementary Education: Music Recordings (cassettes, CDs)
Rhythmically Walking (cassettes)
Guide to Rhythmically Moving 1
Guide to Rhythmically Moving 2

Related High/Scope Press Publications

A School Administrator's Guide to Early Childhood Programs
High/Scope Buyer's Guide to Children's Software, Eleventh Edition
Young Children & Computers
Learning Through Construction
Learning Through Sewing and Pattern Design

Available from
HIGH/SCOPE PRESS

600 North River Street, Ypsilanti, Michigan 48198-2898
ORDERS: Phone (800) 40-PRESS Fax (800) 442-4FAX

FRANK F. BLACKWELL

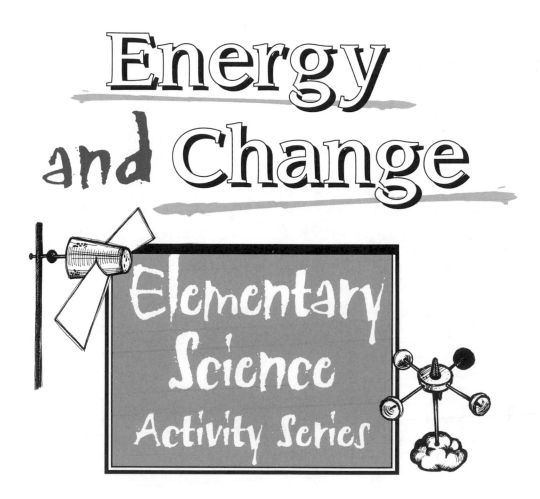

Energy and Change

Elementary Science Activity Series

Series Consultant: ANN S. EPSTEIN

HIGH/SCOPE PRESS
YPSILANTI, MICHIGAN

Published by
HIGH/SCOPE® PRESS

A division of
High/Scope Educational Research Foundation
600 North River Street
Ypsilanti, Michigan 48198-2898
313/485-2000, Fax 313/485-0704

Copyright © 1996 by High/Scope Educational Research Foundation. All rights reserved. No part of this book may be reproduced or transmitted in any form or by any means, electronic or mechanical, including photocopy and recording, or any information storage-and-retrieval system, without permission in writing from the publisher. High/Scope is a registered trademark and service mark of the High/Scope Educational Research Foundation.

Editor: Marcia LaBrenz
Cover and Text Design: Linda Eckel
Illustrations: Lily Taylor

Library of Congress Cataloging-in-Publication Data
Blackwell, Frank.
    Elementary science activity series / by Frank Blackwell.
      p. cm.
    Includes index.
    Contents: 3. Energy and change.
    ISBN 1-57379-011-7 (v. 3)
      1. Science—Study and teaching (Elementary)—United States—Activity programs. I. Title.
LB 1585.3.B53 1996
372.3'5—dc20   96-6806
                                                  CIP

Printed in the United States of America

10 9 8 7 6 5 4 3 2 1

To Mary

In memory of her constant encouragement and support

Contents

List of Illustrations

Appendix I: Teaching Aids

Acknowledgments

The author would like to thank Mr. Charles Wallgren, Executive
Vice President, High/Scope Educational Research Foundation, for
his encouragement and support, and Dr. Ann Epstein, Senior Research
Associate, for her insightful help throughout the production of the
manuscripts. Thanks also to the High/Scope Press editorial staff for
their work in seeing the books through the production process.

Overview of the
Elementary Science Activity Series

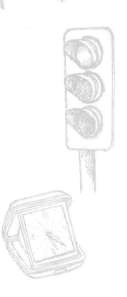

The Process of Science in Elementary Education

Science, in the context of education, is a way of thinking and working in the pursuit of answers to problems about the world in which we live. For children, this pursuit is most often about their immediate concerns, either in material or experiential terms, or both. In fact, hands-on experience is the vehicle for science education in the elementary stage. Throughout their daily lives, children have experiences—often first-time experiences—that reflect their environment and their contacts with it. Children's experiences can, and frequently do, bring into sharp focus even the smallest components of the world around them. This revelation process is as random as it is fortuitous. In addition to these relatively unpredictable sources of children's insights, there also will be opportunities for learning that the teacher deliberately creates for children. These opportunities can be loosely structured, as on a field trip, or more precisely arranged, as in a planned classroom activity.

Whatever the source of these experiences, however, the insights gained will remain as diffuse and unrelated items of knowledge unless the teacher helps children to see the patterns in these fragments. This process—building knowledge from individual observations and insights—is what defines science. With proper guidance and encouragement from the teacher, children in the elementary grades will see how different elements can be fitted together to illuminate their knowledge of, and understanding about, the world in which they live.

Developing a Contemporary Approach to Science Education

Science in education first appeared as a body of knowledge about certain phenomena, or as studies of the structure and form of materials. Using this base, the early science curriculum emphasized the teaching of three general content areas: *physics* was associated with heat, light and sound, and electricity and magnetism; *chemistry* focused on the analysis of substances and on transformations and changes; and *biology* was mainly a descriptive science, concerned with dissection, classification, and identification. This view of science continued until the middle 1950s and early 1960s, when it was largely put aside in favor of a new view of science as a process. Instead of being

built around content, science education now began to emphasize learning through an active discovery process, in which children gained firsthand experiences of many aspects of the world. The tidy content boxes of the past were set aside.

One consequence of these changes for the nonspecialist, however, was a growing sense of bewilderment concerning science. The subject seemed to have little pattern or coherence and rapidly became a fragmented set of experiences. Educators felt they had lost their basis for planning and structuring the science component of the classroom curriculum. On the one hand, they were able to recognize that this new process approach to science was appropriate; children worked on a discovery basis quite naturally. On the other hand, teachers needed some new headings under which the vast array of science knowledge could be organized and made meaningful. Furthermore, the entire discovery process required a broader framework that would relate all elementary learning experiences to the development of thinking skills. In other words, as children developed their observational and analytical skills, teachers needed a sense of when children were in fact acting as true scientists intent on discovering the complexities of their environment.

The High/Scope approach to education is especially suited to giving reality to the teacher's function of "putting children's work into a meaningful relationship with science activities." Posing questions, providing materials and activities, and encouraging a discover-for-yourself approach are essential attributes of the High/Scope classroom, of science education in general, and of the scientific method itself. The High/Scope curriculum for elementary education provides teachers with both a general framework for understanding how children learn and with a specific framework for understanding the role of science education in children's development. With the High/Scope Elementary Curriculum as a reference point, teachers can see how each specific activity contributes to the overall goals of science education and to the general development of children's thinking skills. To be most useful, the High/Scope elementary science curriculum should be

1. Generic in content—exploring broad areas of investigation rather than isolated topics

2. Open in its interpretation—allowing students to observe and analyze what they see instead of internalizing the teacher's explanation

3. Nonprescriptive in its age-related demands—relating activities to children's developmental levels rather than to their specific age

This series of elementary science books presents a wealth of ideas for science activities for the elementary school teacher. Each book in the series serves as a detailed starting point for various classroom activities. Eventually, drawing on their basic understanding of the High/Scope approach and the lessons they have learned from implementing the activities in these books, teachers will be able to develop their own ideas and to enrich the course of science education for their students and themselves.

The High/Scope Approach to Science Education

A guiding principle of the High/Scope Curriculum is the belief that young children are capable of making decisions and solving problems about activities that are interesting to them. Teachers use these individual interests as the springboard for teaching the social and academic concepts that children need to be successful in our society. Another central tenet of the High/Scope approach is the idea of "developmental validity"—the belief that children develop in predictable sequences, that there are optimal times for particular kinds of learning, and that there are teaching methods that are more appropriate at certain times in the developmental sequence than others.

High/Scope's developmental perspective on science learning means that the emphasis is on **stages, not ages.** Children in any one grade level will be at various stages of development; additionally, some children will be at more than one stage in different aspects of science work. Although children progress through the stages in the same general sequence, the rate of progress varies from child to child. Some children will remain at the early stages longer than others; some may never achieve the later stages.

Based on research and knowledge of the developmental patterns typical of how children learn, the High/Scope educational approach has made **active learning** its cornerstone. "Active learning" is learning initiated by the child rather than information handed down or transmitted by the teacher. An activity involves active learning if it includes the following five ingredients:

- *Materials.* A variety of interesting materials are readily accessible to children.

- *Manipulation.* Children are free to handle, explore, and work with the materials.

- *Choice.* Children have opportunities to set their own goals and to select materials and activities.

- *Language from the children.* Children talk about what they are doing and what they have done.

- *Support from adults.* Adults encourage children's efforts and help them extend or build upon their work by talking with them about what they are doing, by asking open-ended questions, by joining them in their activities, and by helping them solve problems that arise.

The High/Scope Curriculum therefore advocates an activity-based science curriculum that stresses active-learning experiences—experiences such as making collections; conducting surveys; building and modifying structures; and representing such experiences in pictures, graphs, and writing. In the High/Scope Elementary Curriculum, teachers are encouraged to provide a **classroom environment that is rich in materials for children's hands-on activities.** The classroom environment and teaching approach are designed to stimulate exploring, discovering, comparing, combining, constructing, and representing activities that are the external reflections of the child's inward construction of knowledge.

Science starts with careful observations and with the use of logical thinking skills to organize and interpret these observations. Science is both a spontaneous and a planned activity, one that depends not only on careful measurement and systematic experimentation but also on the readiness to learn from trial and error, from guesswork, and from serendipity. As emphasized throughout this overview, these basic science processes are simply extensions of children's natural inclination to learn about the world through direct observation and manipulation of materials.

While children engage in this active process, the role of the teacher is to help focus the child's efforts to answer questions and solve problems. In order to make science an active process, the teacher uses **six groups of key experiences for science learning.** "Key experiences" are broadly defined activities and processes that use the important intellectual, social, and physical abilities emerging in children throughout the elementary school years. The six science key experiences describe scientific activity as it is experienced by the children themselves as they observe, experiment, and create explanations for what they see and do.

The six groups of key experiences in the High/Scope Elementary Curriculum are as follows:

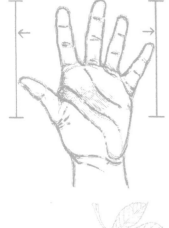

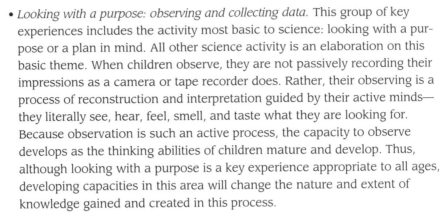

- *Looking with a purpose: observing and collecting data.* This group of key experiences includes the activity most basic to science: looking with a purpose or a plan in mind. All other science activity is an elaboration on this basic theme. When children observe, they are not passively recording their impressions as a camera or tape recorder does. Rather, their observing is a process of reconstruction and interpretation guided by their active minds—they literally see, hear, feel, smell, and taste what they are looking for. Because observation is such an active process, the capacity to observe develops as the thinking abilities of children mature and develop. Thus, although looking with a purpose is a key experience appropriate to all ages, developing capacities in this area will change the nature and extent of knowledge gained and created in this process.

- *Classifying and ordering materials according to their attributes and properties.* This group of key experiences describes children's use of logical thinking skills to organize observations and findings into meaningful groups. The processes of classifying and ordering are fundamental to science. When children notice attributes or structural patterns in living and nonliving materials and then group or order these materials accordingly, they are developing a better understanding of the relationships among materials, organisms, and events in their environment.

- *Measuring, testing, and analyzing: assessing the properties and composition of materials.* In this group of key experiences, children use systematic procedures to make their senses more acute and their observations more precise. These related procedures enable children to quantify the properties and attributes of objects and materials, to express similarities and differences in numeric terms, and to describe cause-effect relationships quantitatively. As they use these basic techniques, children gain a deeper understanding not only of the materials they are examining, but also of the importance of careful assessment.

- *Observing, predicting, and controlling change: understanding causality.* While the previous groups of key experiences mainly involve ways of measuring materials systematically, this group focuses on causes. Here again, children are organizing and interpreting their observations, but the focus is on inter–action and change rather than fixed attributes. As children notice and describe sequences of events in the world, they begin to notice regular patterns of change. This leads them to the heart of scientific inquiry: the effort to explain the causes behind the phenomena of nature.

- *Designing, building, fabricating, and modifying structures or materials.* In this group of key experiences, children apply scientific knowledge as they solve real-life problems. Working in this practical vein, children develop their understanding of fundamental physical causes. The building projects that children undertake can range from the simple to the complex, and can include projects of the teacher's design as well as inventions that are completely child-initiated. As they work through the processes in this group of key experiences, children begin to learn the reasons for observable changes in the position, motion, shape, and size of objects and materials. They begin to understand how objects interact by pushing, pulling, holding, and bumping one another, and they begin to see how they can exert some control over these events by manipulating the factors involved.

- *Reporting and interpreting data and results.* In this group of key experiences, children use language, pictures, and mathematical symbols to represent, and thus communicate, their observations and findings. Representation serves the practical and essential scientific function of sharing results with others. Engaging in this recording process also helps children sharpen their observations and clarify their thinking.

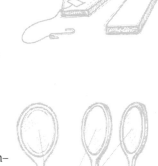

Taken together with the content themes and activities in this series of elementary science books, the key experiences provide a process-oriented framework that teachers can use to focus children's science learning. Keeping the key experiences in mind helps the teacher recognize and build on the valuable scientific activity children engage in spontaneously as they explore the world.

Three Major Curriculum Areas in Science Education

The following three curriculum areas contain the principal elements needed to develop an approach to science education: **life and environment, structure and form,** and **energy and change.** These three areas, which correspond to the three books in the High/Scope elementary science series, provide a framework for embracing all of the major themes of science. They also provide a framework for organizing the diverse opportunities for science work that will arise in any classroom. With an insight into some of the ideas associated with these generic headings, teachers can determine what science is about in the context of their own work in the classroom. Furthermore, this broad framework should help teach-ers put children's science work into a more meaningful relationship with other educational activities throughout the curriculum.

The lists that follow describe the specific subthemes included within each of the three main curriculum areas in the High/Scope elementary science books. These should not be viewed as definitive lists but rather as working ones that can be changed by teachers to suit their specific circumstances and the children's emerging interests. An advantage of using a broad, thematically based list is its compatibility with a wide range of other currently available print and audiovisual science education material. These additional resources can be used to supplement and enrich the activities described in the High/Scope elementary science series. As these themes and activities are used in the ele-mentary school classroom, however, teachers should always keep in mind the High/Scope emphasis on active learning and developmental stages rather than passive and age-defined instruction.

Major Curriculum Areas and Subthemes in High/Scope Elementary Science Education

Life and Environment

The Environment Is Where You Are
Moving in an Environment
Communication Between Environments
Your Environment: Beneath Your Feet
Your Environment: On the Walls
Your Environment: Above Your Head
Taking Care of Our Environment
Basic Materials for Supporting the Study of Living Things in the Environment

Collecting, Collections, and the Environment
Looking at Living Forms in the Environment
Food for Life From Living Forms
Animals in the Environment: Invertebrates and Vertebrates

Structure and Form

Triangles
Structures Around Us
Structures for Fastening
Natural Structures and Forms
Structure, Size, Symmetry, and Shape
Structure and Patterns
The Structural Properties of Materials
Skin: A Living Structure
The Structure of Everyday Items in the Science Context
Common Textbook Topics on Structure From a New Perspective

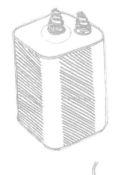

Energy and Change

Using Gravity
Energy From the Air: Wind Energy
Human Energy
Sound Energy
Heat Energy
Weather
Change in the Garden
Diversity in Change
Electrical Energy
Magnets and Magnetism

How the Books Are Organized

The High/Scope Elementary Curriculum science books are organized into three volumes, one for each of the major content areas: **life and environment, structure and form, and energy and change.** Within each volume, various activities are described for each of the subthemes listed above. Included with each activity is a standard set of information designed to help teachers determine the activity's appropriateness for their students, plan its implementation, and help children focus on a range of exciting and relevant learning experiences. The following information accompanies each activity:

- *Developmental level.* For each activity, the appropriate developmental level is suggested. As noted above, these levels are based on stages rather than ages. Because there is wide variation within and across any group of children, developmental levels are given according to a three-grade span: K–2, 1–3, 2–4, 3–5, and 4–6. Some activities are complex and allow variations that span more than one developmental level; these increasing levels of developmental complexity are also indicated in the text.

- *Group size.* Each activity specifies whether it is suitable for a large or a small group. Although traditional classrooms generally involve all of the students in the same activity at the same time, the High/Scope approach advocates a balance of large- and small-group activity. Some activities are suitable for the entire class, such as a field trip to observe the plant and animal wildlife around the school building. Other activities allow for more intense interaction and varied approaches to the same problem if they are carried out in small groups. In both situations, children may work independently, in pairs, or in a variety of other combinations. Teachers may circulate among individuals and groups to provide encouragement, ask open-ended questions, and observe the children's interests with an eye toward planning future activities. In both large and small groups, children should be given ample opportunity to share their observations, questions, hypotheses, and results with one another as well as with the teacher.

- *Key experiences.* Each activity lists the relevant key experience group or groups to help teachers focus children as they observe, explore, manipulate, and analyze materials. Most activities allow students to engage in more than one of the six science key experiences. Teachers should also be aware that unanticipated questions and spontaneous pursuits by individual students may provide an opportunity to draw out key experiences in addition to those listed here.

- *Notes to teachers.* Some activities include inset notes to teachers. These notes serve two purposes. First, they provide background information on topics about which teachers may have limited experience or knowledge themselves. Second, they provide additional information on topics that students may choose to explore in greater depth. Again, teachers are reminded that there is a wealth of science resource material available for classroom use. These notes are meant to illustrate that with some simple research and follow-through, teachers and students can pursue their interests and expand their science knowledge with confidence.

Following the specific activities within each volume is a section titled "Case Studies: Some Classroom Experiences." These case studies are drawn from the author's experiences in implementing science activities with groups of students. They are included to emphasize that science education is indeed a learning process, that what one has planned going into an activity may evolve in a series of other directions depending on the children's understanding and interest. For each classroom example, the author provides a lively discussion of general experiences the teacher had in mind, other experiences the teacher hoped to encourage, follow-up activities the teacher hoped to stimulate, and the activities that actually resulted. Reading these classroom experiences will help teachers gain an appreciation of active learning, the process children engage in as they shape their own activities and create their own knowledge. The case studies should also give teachers confidence to use the activities in these books as a starting point on which spontaneous happenings can build. Things may not go as planned, but a flexible teacher can ensure that learning will always occur.

Finally, each of the three volumes concludes with two appendixes:

- *Appendix I: Teaching Aids.* The first appendix provides teachers with some general ideas about how to carry out science education. It contains the following sections: (a) communication techniques for the classroom; (b) materials and equipment; (c) measurement in science (measurement techniques/simple devices and the metric system); (d) testing and analysis; and (e) safety and science.

- *Appendix II: The Development of Problem-Solving Skills.* Because science is a process of discovery and seeking answers to questions, this appendix explains the stages of development in children's problem-solving skills.

The information will be helpful to teachers as they select activities and adapt them to the developmental levels and skills of individuals and groups in the classroom.

As in all activities within the High/Scope Elementary Curriculum, science learning is seen as an active process of doing and experiencing, rather than a passive one of absorbing information presented by the teacher. Yet the fact that students are active by no means implies that teachers play a lesser role in children's learning. On the contrary, the more active the students, the more active and flexible teachers must be in creating the learning environment, in responding to children's observations and questions, and in building upon children's expanding interests. The High/Scope Elementary Curriculum allows teachers to learn and explore along with their students. Science education becomes a process of mutual discovery that can be as exciting for adults as it is for children.

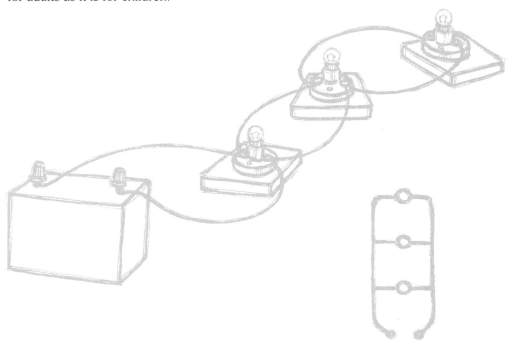

► *Introduction to Book 3*
Energy and Change

Energy and **change** are important concepts in our scientific study of the world. Our entire universe, in fact, is a product of the interactions between energy and matter, and energy in one form or another pervades all of our lives. There are many sources of energy, such as gravity, wind, sound, heat, light, electricity, and magnetic force. Human beings can also be an energy source. Although energy can be neither created nor destroyed, it can change form. Many opportunities exist for studying changes in energy. Our changing weather, for example, is an interesting topic for young students to explore, as are changes in the growth of flowers in a garden and in the growth of human beings. Although energy is in many ways a complex subject to study, children can be introduced to many simple elements of energy and matter.

What Is Energy?

In physics, *energy* is defined as "the property of a system that diminishes when it does work on another system." An important law in physics—the Law of the Conservation of Energy—states that the amount of energy in the universe is always the same; it can be neither increased nor decreased. Although energy cannot be created or destroyed, it can be developed from matter and turned into matter. *Matter* consists of particles. Substances differ one from another because their particles are arranged differently. Understanding energy and matter—the two fundamental principles of physics—helps to give meaning to the new discoveries of present-day scientists.

It may be helpful to review some of the technical terms connected with the study of energy, especially as these terms have been defined in conventional textbooks. Most often *energy* is defined as "the ability to do work." Work and energy can be measured in the same units. People often confuse the term *energy* with the terms *force* or *power*. *Force* can be broadly described as "a push or a pull." The amount of work is determined by the strength of the force used and the distance through which it moves. *Power,* on the other hand, measures the rate at which the work is done.

What Are the Types and Sources of Energy?

In thinking about energy it is useful to think about it in two forms—potential energy and kinetic energy. *Potential energy* can be thought of as stored energy. It represents work that has already been done in some way. A ball or a rock lodged on top of a hill has potential energy. The ball or the rock had to be put into its place—by nature or by humans—to give it potential energy. When the ball or rock starts to move down the hill its potential energy becomes *kinetic energy*. Kinetic energy is the energy of movement. The word *kinetic* comes from the Greek word meaning "to move." Energy is constantly changing from the potential to the kinetic state, and this process is referred to as the *transformation of energy.*

Energy occurs in convertible forms—that is, energy is capable of being changed from one form into another. It is these outward manifestations of change that children can readily investigate and from which real discoveries about energy can be made. For example, energy can come from chemical changes, such as burning. Falling objects have an energy brought about by gravitational force. A waterfall provides energy that can generate electricity or run a simple water wheel. Some energy comes from heat. Other sources of energy include light and even sound.

How Can Elementary-Aged Children Grasp the Concept of Energy?

By focusing science activities on the visible signs of energy—how it accomplishes work, how it changes from one form to another—teachers can help children appreciate the fundamentals of something as complex as energy. Children can also be introduced to the concept of *energy conservation,* an important consideration as the world consumes increasing reserves of finite energy resources. Elementary-aged children will appreciate the importance of conserving energy as they discover ways in which *they* may help conserve our earth's resources. For example, better insulation of buildings, small reductions in room temperature, and fluorescent lighting are all ways in which energy can be saved in our homes and in our schools. Smaller cars, greater use of public transportation, and more recycling of used materials can also produce huge energy savings in our daily lives. By exploring the role of energy in different environments—home, school, office, and recreational settings—teachers can help children to understand how energy pervades their everyday lives.

3 1833 03961 2103

Using Gravity

E nergy from falling objects—using gravitational force—is the principle behind many simple toys that children play with at home and at school. Children have a natural interest in movement, not only in how things move but also in the speed and the power of movement. The following activities use such simple items as bouncing balls and playground slides to introduce children to the basic principles of gravity.

Rolling Balls ► *Activity 1*

DEVELOPMENTAL LEVEL
K–2

GROUP SIZE
Small

KEY EXPERIENCES

- *Measuring, testing, and analyzing: assessing the properties and composition of materials*

- *Observing, predicting, and controlling change: understanding causality*

- *Designing, building, fabricating, and modifying structures or materials*

Children's natural interest in collisions often is evident in their early play with toy cars and balls and other items. Here is an activity that lets children put that interest to scientific use. Children can make a simple slope from a length of plastic guttering placed on a stack of books (see Illustration 1). Begin with a stack of six books. A ball is rolled down the slope to collide with a block at the bottom. Will the block move? Does the ball have enough energy to move two blocks? Or three blocks?

What happens if only three books are stacked at the top of the slope? What if nine books are used? Have students put a hand in place of the block and feel the ball hit from three books high, then six, and finally nine. Then go back to three books to make the comparison. Falling objects have energy changes as they move from a higher place to a lower one.

Children can experience this same phenomenon firsthand on the playground slide. Have one child go to the top and release a ball for another to receive on its arrival at the bottom. Then have the child at the top descend slowly to the halfway point of the slide and release the ball again to the receiver (see Illustration 2 on pg. 13). Ask the receiver to feel the force of the ball's arrival at the bottom. Which force is greater—the force of the ball from the top or from halfway?

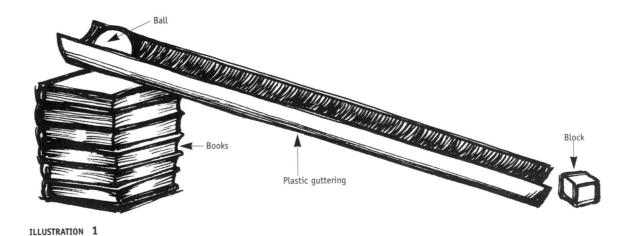

Ball

Books

Plastic guttering

Block

ILLUSTRATION 1

The Energy of Moving Objects

Children can put their interest in collisions to use in this simple experiment in which a ball is rolled down a slope to collide with an object below.

To begin, one child releases a
ball from the top of the slide.

Next, the child slowly descends halfway down
the slide and releases the ball again.

ILLUSTRATION 2

Gravitational Force and Falling Objects
Children can investigate elements of gravitational force in this simple experiment on the playground slide.

Constructing a Standard Test Apparatus
for Gravity ▶ *Activity 2*

Students can make a roller coaster from a length of flexible, light-weight plastic (for example, a plastic curtain rod); a lightweight glass marble and a heavier metal ball bearing; and standard building units of the same size, such as books, house bricks, or wooden blocks (see Illustration 3).

The roller coaster can be used by children to solve simple energy problems. For example: If A is higher than C and the marble or ball is released at A, will it reach C? What happens if C is higher than A? What effect does the height of B have on the travel of the marble or ball?

DEVELOPMENTAL LEVEL
K–2

GROUP SIZE
Small

KEY EXPERIENCES

- *Measuring, testing, and analyzing: assessing the properties and composition of materials*

- *Observing, predicting, and controlling change: understanding causality*

- *Designing, building, fabricating, and modifying structures or materials*

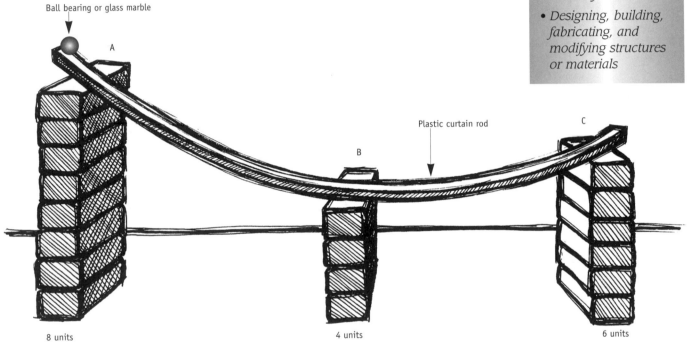

Ball bearing or glass marble

A

Plastic curtain rod

B

C

8 units

4 units

6 units

ILLUSTRATION **3**

Creating a Device for Investigating Gravity
Students can construct a simple roller coaster to explore and solve various energy problems.

Constructing a Standard Test Apparatus for Gravity ▶ *Activity 3*

DEVELOPMENTAL LEVEL
2–4

GROUP SIZE
Small

KEY EXPERIENCES

- *Measuring, testing, and analyzing: assessing the properties and composition of materials*

- *Observing, predicting, and controlling change: understanding causality*

- *Designing, building, fabricating, and modifying structures or materials*

Children in grades 2–4 can build on the basic ideas introduced in Activity 2 by experimenting with different designs—different heights for A, B, and C (see Illustration 3 on pg. 14). The test at each height should be repeated three times to allow for natural variation. They can then compare the results of using the heavy ball bearing with the lighter marble and record their results on a chart such as the one below.

The Effects of Height and Weight on Gravitational Force

Location along Roller Coaster	Height (Number of Units)	Ball Bearing			Marble		
		Test #1	Test #2	Test #3	Test #1	Test #2	Test #3
A							
B							
C							

Constructing a Standard Test Apparatus
for Gravity ► *Activity 4*

Students in grades 4 to 6 can build even further on the ideas introduced in the previous two activities. Teachers should keep in mind, however, that these students may vary greatly in their understanding of the basic principles of energy. Some may be just developing an experiential awareness of energy, while others may be ready for such concepts as the relative changes in the energy of position and the energy of movement. Using a device such as the one in Illustration 3 on page 14, teachers can introduce new concepts to students by helping them develop activities to answer questions such as the following:

• Where does the ball have energy of position?

• Where does it have energy of movement?

• If the ball is stopped at B, can it achieve energy of movement to return to A or go on to C?

To answer these and other questions, children can construct roller coasters by bringing in toys from home or by using apparatus in the classroom.

DEVELOPMENTAL LEVEL
4–6

GROUP SIZE
Small

KEY EXPERIENCES

• *Measuring, testing, and analyzing: assessing the properties and composition of materials*

• *Observing, predicting, and controlling change: understanding causality*

• *Designing, building, fabricating, and modifying structures or materials*

• *Reporting and interpreting data and results*

Bouncing Balls ► *Activity 5*

DEVELOPMENTAL LEVEL
K–2

GROUP SIZE
Small

KEY EXPERIENCES

• *Measuring, testing, and analyzing: assessing the properties and composition of materials*

• *Observing, predicting, and controlling change: understanding causality*

• *Designing, building, fabricating, and modifying structures or materials*

—— A NOTE FOR TEACHERS ——

Bouncing

Some children will appreciate that bouncing can be explained in terms of energy. If both the ball and the surface it is bounced on are physically similar, the bounce is immediate and high. If the bouncing causes changes in the shape of the ball or the surface, then the bounce is poor. Energy is used in changing the shape of the ball and in denting the ball or the bouncing surface. Energy is also used if the dent in the ball has to be pushed out again. This use of energy is very apparent when bouncing modeling clay or when trying to bounce items on sand or on a soft cushion. In addition, kinetic energy is also lost when balls are bounced as this energy is changed into sound energy and very small amounts of heat energy. If too much energy is lost, the ball will not bounce at all. Sometimes a ball does not bounce well because it does not return to its original shape quickly enough.

Keeping these principles in mind, there are many other investigations that children can explore:

• How does the bouncing of rubber balls of different types compare? Is it size that influences bounce the most or other qualities? How high does the ball bounce? How will this be measured? How many times does it bounce before losing all its energy and coming to rest? Have students make a chart to record their answers.

• How many things can be changed to alter the bounce of balls? Have students study the bounce of a heavy marble or a ball bearing. What surfaces will be tested? How will the bounce be measured? Does the surface change after the bounce? Is there any relationship between the height of the bounce and any surface changes? Are there obvious differences in the properties of the surfaces on which the ball bearing bounces well and the ones on which it bounces badly?

To begin this activity, have a wide selection of different types of balls available, such as tennis balls, golf balls, table tennis (Ping-Pong) balls, soccer balls, beach balls, plastic lightweight balls, small, high-bouncing balls, and balls of yarn. Pose the following questions to students:

• Which kind of ball bounces best? How do you know? What would be a simple way to test this? How can the test be made fair?

• Does size matter? Does color?

• Which ball bounces the most times before it comes to rest?

Students can test the bouncing capacity of various types of balls by rolling them off the end of a table onto a bare floor or wooden surface. Have them try a marble, a golf ball, a tennis ball, and a table tennis (Ping-Pong) ball. Try to introduce some greater accuracy into the experiment by propping a ruler against the table or by pinning a card with a scale on it over the table's edge (see Illustration 4). Students can record the results on graphs or in diagrams.

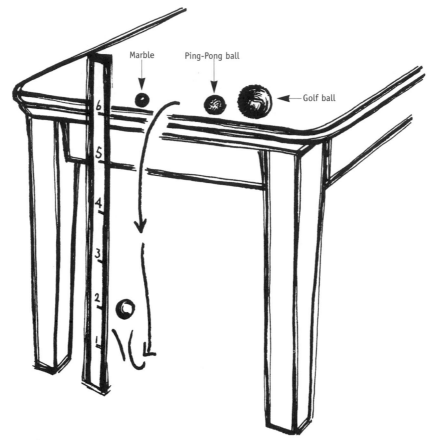

Marble   Ping-Pong ball

Golf ball

6

5

4

3

2

1

ILLUSTRATION 4

How High Does a Ball Bounce?

By propping a ruler or yardstick against a table, students can measure the bouncing capacities of various types of balls.

Bouncing Balls ▶ *Activity 6*

Using the same materials and setup as for grades K–2, the work can be carried through more exactingly with children in grades 2–4. Students can explore the question: Is one measurement enough? They can use the scale to observe more accurately and to record the results. Let them take five readings to become aware of the variability in their observations; then find the average. Students can set out the results—first in table form, next in block graph form, and finally as a statement on the bouncing capacity of each ball.

DEVELOPMENTAL LEVEL
2–4

GROUP SIZE
Small

KEY EXPERIENCES

• *Measuring, testing, and analyzing: assessing the properties and composition of materials*

• *Observing, predicting, and controlling change: understanding causality*

• *Designing, building, fabricating, and modifying structures or materials*

• *Reporting and interpreting data and results*

Bouncing Balls ▶ *Activity 7*

DEVELOPMENTAL LEVEL
4–6

GROUP SIZE
Small

KEY EXPERIENCES

• *Measuring, testing, and analyzing: assessing the properties and composition of materials*

• *Observing, predicting, and controlling change: understanding causality*

• *Designing, building, fabricating, and modifying structures or materials*

• *Reporting and interpreting data and results*

Using the same materials and setup as in grades 2–4, students in grades 4–6 can begin this activity by carrying out the test and recording the results. They can then try a variety of other surfaces for the balls to fall on, such as a piece of carpet or mat, foam rubber, sand, a piece of plastic, and a thick cushion (see Illustration 5). Students can record the results in exactly the same manner as they did for the first set and then make comparisons. Some questions that may arise include the following:

• Does the height of the bounce depend on the cleanliness or smoothness of the surface?

• Is bounce related to the firmness of the surface?

• On which surface do the balls bounce best? Worst? How can you describe the surfaces and their differential effects on bouncing?

ILLUSTRATION 5

How High Do Balls Bounce on Different Surfaces?

After testing how well balls bounce on various surfaces, encourage students to describe the surfaces and their differential effects on bouncing.

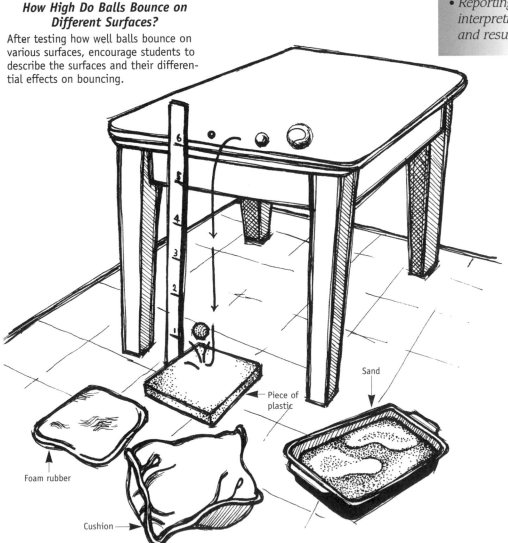

Foam rubber

Cushion

Piece of plastic

Sand

Energy and Slopes on the Playground ► *Activity 8*

DEVELOPMENTAL LEVEL
K–2

GROUP SIZE
Large

KEY EXPERIENCES

- *Measuring, testing, and analyzing: assessing the properties and composition of materials*

- *Observing, predicting, and controlling change: understanding causality*

- *Reporting and interpreting data and results*

Children's games on a playground slide can be put to use in science. If a doll is allowed to slide from the top, for example, how far from the end does it go? Which position seems to give the doll the most energy in getting to the end of the slide? Let children experience the results for themselves by descending on the slide first from halfway, then from the top. Can they feel the differences in reaching the end of the slide from each of these two spots?

A playground slide provides a natural slope on which children can test the energy of various vehicles. A variety of vehicles can be tried, ranging from small homemade wheeled toys to fast running toy cars. Is there any pattern to the results? Talk about the experiments using the children's personal experiences as the basis of discussion. For these types of playground activities, talking will be most useful way to communicate.

Children can continue their investigations in the classroom. They can construct simple slopes made from a 4-foot (1 ½ meter) plank supported by bricks, blocks, or books of equal size. This basic apparatus allows for plenty of innovative, investigative activity into the controlled use of the energy of falling objects.

Timing and Gravity ► *Activity 9*

DEVELOPMENTAL LEVEL
1–3

GROUP SIZE
Small

KEY EXPERIENCES

• *Measuring, testing, and analyzing: assessing the properties and composition of materials*

• *Observing, predicting, and controlling change: understanding causality*

• *Designing, building, fabricating, and modifying structures or materials*

• *Reporting and interpreting data and results*

A NOTE FOR TEACHERS

Time—Its Appreciation and Measurement

Children initially measure and order time by the sequence of events. While the invisible flow of time is difficult for young children to appreciate, they know the rhythms imposed by school and family routines. Time as a rhythm or a repeated pattern is better comprehended by children, and they can use this understanding as a way to measure time. However, the concept of time as a "duration" is less easily understood. The relationship of time to a clock face is only fully appreciated by children who realize that the passing of time is measured by the rotation of the hands—quite a sophisticated concept.

At first, time is not quantitative for children; it is a stream of present and past events. It is only later in the elementary school years that different scales for the measurement of time can be fully coordinated and set in relation to each other. When children use time as a measure of performance (for example, the amount of time it takes to complete a task), indicators that move quickly enough to be easily noticed are the most helpful. The seconds hand of a clock or watch, the ticking of a kitchen timer, or the passage of sand in an egg timer are all useful devices for measuring time. The different but regular repeating rhythms that children encounter in music can also help to establish the idea of measurable time. The metronome, with its clear tick, is also a good visual embodiment of the idea of a "second." Using measuring devices such as these, children can measure how far they can run, hop, skip, walk, and jump in half a minute; they can count how many times a ball bounces in a given time. Using objective intervals of time to measure activities and experiments will help to establish the objectivity of time and disassociate it from speed.

The idea that time can be divided into equal units and be measured is a sophisticated concept. An even more sophisticated concept is the idea of the measurement of speed. The connection between time, speed, and distance calls for a coordination of three variables and is beyond the developmental stages of most young children. It is later, as the idea of time develops, that children are able to understand and measure what "faster" means. But during that time they are developing an appreciation, through real activities, of the idea of measurement. In the later grades of elementary school, measuring will be understood and related to rates of change and distance.

Children enjoy running toy cars down slopes. Teachers can build on this natural interest to introduce children to various timing activities. For example, children can time the descent of cars over a fixed distance and for different heights of slope. The slopes can be built with stacks of 2, 3, 4, or 5 units of bricks or books. Timing can be done first by counting to a set pattern; for example, the children can count "1 and 2 and 3 and 4" and so on. Students can then use a simple timing device, such as a sand or water clock. Sand or water clocks can be made from a plastic squeeze bottle with the bottom cut off and with water or sand running into a jar put below it. (**Note:** If sand is used it must be very dry and very fine. First run it through a kitchen sieve.) Students can then mark or graduate the jar by counting and sticking a strip on to mark the scale (see Illustration 6). It does not matter how the scale is graduated as long as the same measuring device is used every time. (Discuss the idea of using standardized measures with the children.) Students can record the results of the tests in various ways, such as by making block graphs.

Students can try different variations to explore which conditions affect how much time it takes for the toy cars to reach the bottom of the slope. For example, the effect of cleaning the wheels and of sparingly oiling the bearings can be measured. If the cars have rubber tires, students can see the effect of removing the tires. In each case, students can determine whether changing the conditions improves or worsens performance. The results be charted along with the others already measured.

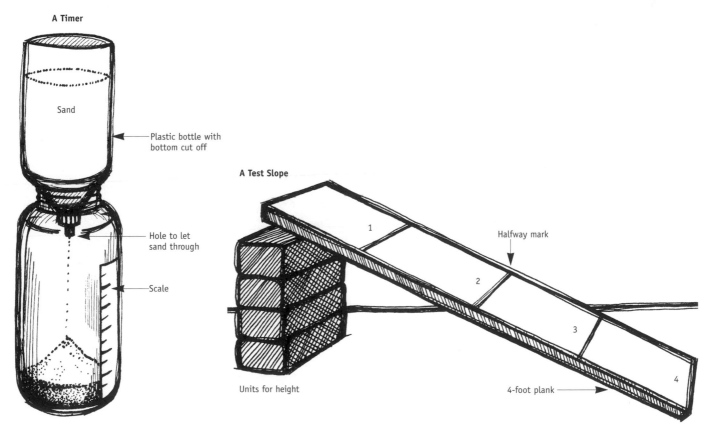

A Timer

Sand

Plastic bottle with bottom cut off

Hole to let sand through

Scale

A Test Slope

1

Halfway mark

2

3

4

Units for height

4-foot plank

ILLUSTRATION **6**

A Simple Timing Activity
After constructing a test slope and a simple timing device, such as a sand clock, students can explore the conditions that affect how long it takes for a toy car to reach the bottom of a slope.

Timing and Gravity ▶ *Activity 10*

To begin this activity, have the materials available as suggested for grades 1–3 and let the students do the experiments as far as they wish. The recording of results should be more precise and the discussion of their implications more focused. Added impetus can be given to work at this level by researching the question: What is the effect on the performance of the cars going down a given slope if weights are added to them? Just as it was necessary to invent a timing device with the younger children, now some weighing device will be essential. An elastic band makes a useful measuring device for this situation. Students can weigh a car by suspending the car from the band and measuring the band's stretch. They can then run the car down the slope, noting its performance. Students can then load the car with a measurable load (such as 1" nails or nuts and bolts of identical sizes) and test the car's performance under various loads. Have the students record and discuss the results.

KEY EXPERIENCES

- *Looking with a purpose: observing and collecting data*

- *Measuring, testing, and analyzing: assessing the properties and composition of materials*

- *Observing, predicting, and controlling change: understanding causality*

- *Designing, building, fabricating, and modifying structures or materials*

- *Reporting and interpreting data and results*

Using a School Table for Collision Tests ►
Activity 11

DEVELOPMENTAL LEVEL
4–6

GROUP SIZE
Small

KEY EXPERIENCES

- *Looking with a purpose: observing and collecting data*

- *Measuring, testing, and analyzing: assessing the properties and composition of materials*

- *Observing, predicting, and controlling change: understanding causality*

- *Designing, building, fabricating, and modifying structures or materials*

- *Reporting and interpreting data and results*

— A NOTE FOR TEACHERS —

Weight and Weighing

Weight is the gravitational force placed on an object by the planet on which it is located. *Gravitational force*, or "gravity," is the natural force of attraction between all objects because of their mass. *Mass* can be defined as the amount of matter in an object, although scientists now usually use a more complicated definition connecting inertia and resistance to acceleration. However, for elementary school purposes, it is sufficient to consider mass as the amount of matter. Because of gravitation, objects on or near the earth are pulled towards it, and this is called the *force of gravity.* The weight of an object depends on two factors—the distance from the object to the center of the planet and the object's mass. An object's weight is largest if the object is on the surface of the planet. The weight becomes smaller if the object is moved away from the planet. An object will be weightless in space when the gravitational force on it is too weak to be measured. Objects far away from the Earth's surface become weightless at about 210,000 miles or 338,000 kilometers. However, the amount of matter remains unchanged.

Mass and weight are different, although they are often confused with each other. Scales such as the beam balance and the spring balance compare weights, not masses. Both types of scales depend on gravitational pull for their functioning. Space exploration highlights the differences between mass and weight with some interesting figures. A man weighing 200 pounds (91 kilograms) on Earth would weigh only 32 pounds (15 kilograms) on the moon; because the moon is smaller than the earth, its gravitational force is smaller. However, on Jupiter he would weigh 529 pounds (240 kilograms) because the planet is much larger than Earth. The common units for measuring weight are the ounce and the pound. In the metric system, the gram and kilogram are used.

Children will be familiar with collisions of many kinds, including their own falls during play. An interesting series of investigations can be explored around the topic: What accounts for the energy in a crash? Tilt a tabletop by placing bricks, books, or blocks of even size under two legs to provide a slope. The bricks, books, or blocks are the "units" of slope. Mark a starting line on the slope; then 2 feet (or $\frac{1}{2}$ meter) away mark another line as the collision line. Use three tins as vehicles; empty soda pop cans are excellent for this purpose. Students should leave one tin empty, fill the second tin with sawdust or paper pieces, and fill the third tin with sand (see Illustration 7 on pg. 26). (The idea is to get vehicles of light, medium, and heavy weights.) Make sure they seal the filler holes with cellophane tape. Students can make a target vehicle of a matchbox filled with clay or plaster of Paris.

Have students test the energy in the vehicles as follows. Make a 1-unit slope (that is, a slope made with one brick, one book, or one block). Take the target vehicle and put it in the center of the collision line. Put the lightweight vehicle (can) on the starting line and aim it to collide with the target. Release it. Let it roll to collide with the target. If the target is moved, measure how far it is pushed forward by the collision. Then try the medium-weight vehicle. Measure as before and record the results. Finally, try the heavyweight vehicle and measure and record the results.

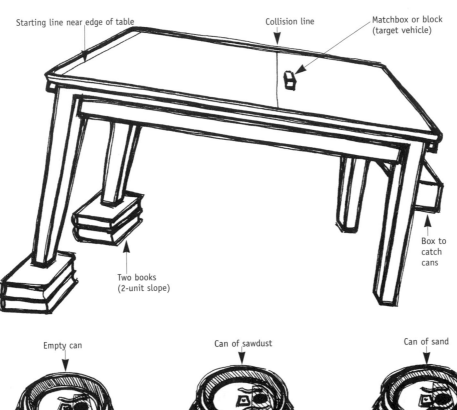

Starting line near edge of table

Collision line

Matchbox or block (target vehicle)

Box to catch cans

Two books (2-unit slope)

ILLUSTRATION 7

How Weight Affects the Energy of Collisions

Using three cans of different weights as test vehicles, students can explore how gravitational force is affected by an object's weight.

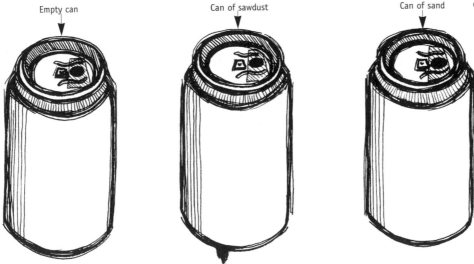

Empty can

Can of sawdust

Can of sand

Next, alter the height of the slope by increasing the number of bricks, books, or blocks. Repeat the experiments with the different weights of vehicles and record the results as before. To get more accurate results, take four readings each time and, with the teacher's assistance, work out the average. Have students set out the results in a table, such as the one below, for discussion.

The Effects of Slope and Weight in the Energy of Collisions

Slope (Number of Units)	Weight of Vehicle	Average Distance Moved				Average Distance Moved
		Reading #1	Reading #2	Reading #3	Reading #4	
Two Units	Light					
	Medium					
	Heavy					
Four Units	Light					
	Medium					
	Heavy					
Six Units	Light					
	Medium					
	Heavy					

Discuss the significance of any differences in energy due to weight and slope. When they review their results, students should be able to answer questions such as these: Which cans roll the fastest, the light or the heavy? Which cans move the target the furthest, the light or the heavy? Are these results the same for different heights of the slope?

► *Part Two*

Energy From the Air: Wind Energy

T he power of moving air is great and its strength can be experienced, measured, and used even by young children. It is an energy source that has been used over the centuries in sailing ships and windmills, as well as in toys such as kites.

Flags in the Air ► *Activity 12*

DEVELOPMENTAL LEVEL
K–2

GROUP SIZE
Large

KEY EXPERIENCES

• *Looking with a purpose: observing and collecting data*

• *Reporting and interpreting data and results*

Students begin this activity by making a series of small flags from rectangles of lightweight nylon material. They can then take their flags to various locations outside and near the school. Have them observe any movements in the flags. What causes this movement? Have them bring the flags indoors and hold them up. Can they make the flags move an equal amount by blowing on them? To make the flags wave, the wind must have at least as much power as the students' blowing.

Making Plastic Bag Kites ► *Activity 13*

DEVELOPMENTAL LEVEL
1–3

GROUP SIZE
Small

KEY EXPERIENCES

• *Observing, predicting, and controlling change: understanding causality*

• *Designing, building, fabricating, and modifying structures or materials*

• *Reporting and interpreting data and results*

Students can try using the energy of the wind to fly a plastic bag kite. This type of kite can be made by fastening a lightweight string at each corner of the mouth of the bag. Bring the strings together in a V shape about 12" (30 cm) from the bag and tie a single long, lightweight string to the other strings. When it is windy, let the wind fill the bag. Feel the power of the wind as it fills the bag and takes it into the air.

Students can hold a kite-flying show using either these homemade kites or kites bought from a toy store. Have them feel how the energy in the wind lifts the kites. Pose questions such as the following: Which kite flies the best? Why? Have students make a list of reasons why some kites fly well and why others do not.

Making a Large Octagon Kite ▶ *Activity 14*

DEVELOPMENTAL LEVEL
4–6

GROUP SIZE
Small

KEY EXPERIENCES

• *Measuring, testing, and analyzing: assessing the properties and composition of materials*

• *Observing, predicting, and controlling change: understanding causality*

• *Designing, building, fabricating, and modifying structures or materials*

• *Reporting and interpreting data and results*

To begin, students make two squares, each with 24" (60 cm) sides, from a lightweight wood, such as balsa or bamboo. They should attach them at the edges with a strong, quick-drying glue. When the glue is dry and really hard, have them fix the corners with cellophane tape as an extra fastening. They should then place one square diagonally over the other, as shown in Illustration 8 on page 33. Next, they should take the top and bottom of one square and tuck them under the upper and lower sides of the other square to interlace them. Have them adjust the squares so that all the surrounding triangles are equal. Finally, they should glue and tie all the joints.

After the two squares are put together, students should tie a 40" (1 meter) center pole as shown in Illustration 8. This pole will be temporary at first as students check the balance of the kite frame by putting the free end of the center pole on the edge of a table and supporting the tip of the kite frame with their finger. If the frame falls to one side or the other, they should balance the pole accordingly. When the center pole is balanced, students should glue and tie it in place.

Next, have students cover the side opposite the center pole (the underside) with a thin sheet of plastic or rice paper cut into an octagon shape. This material should be fastened with a suitable glue. Students can decorate the plastic or paper. Rice paper is easier to decorate than plastic but not as easy to handle when fixing it to the kite frame.

Finally, have students make a tail. It will need to be long—about 6 to 8 feet (2 to 2.5 m)—depending on the strength of the wind. If the tail is too short, the kite will loop and spin; a tail that is too long will "wag the kite." A standard tail can be made by tying strips of thin material each measuring 6" × 2" (15 cm × 5 cm) at 6" intervals (15 cm) down a string. The same type of string used for the flying line, such as household three-ply twine that comes in 250-feet balls, can also be used for the tail. Students should test the performance of the kite in a trial flight and adjust the length of the tail by either cutting a piece off or tying on another. Finally, students should attach the flying bridle, as shown in Illustration 9 on page 33.

Students can make several kites and have a kite fair. Let them experiment with different shapes, tail lengths, and sizes of kites. Have them decorate the kites to differentiate them in the air.

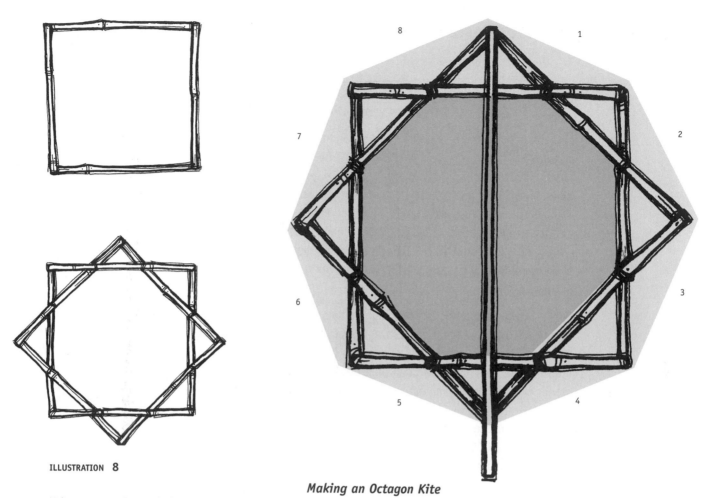

ILLUSTRATION 8

Making an Octagon Kite

Using two squares made from a lightweight wood, students can create an octagon kite. The two squares are overlapped, a center pole is attached down the middle, and a piece of plastic or rice paper is glued onto the kite frame.

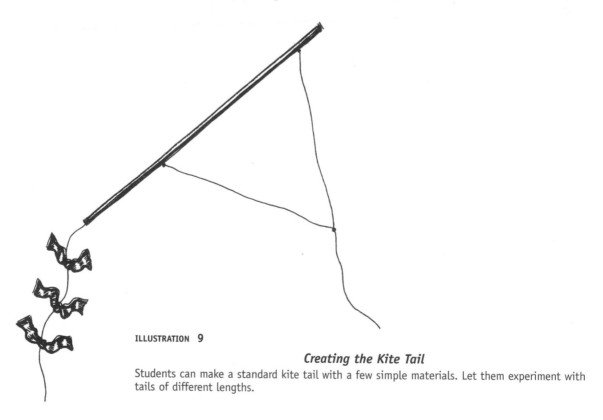

ILLUSTRATION 9

Creating the Kite Tail

Students can make a standard kite tail with a few simple materials. Let them experiment with tails of different lengths.

Windmills ▶ *Activity 15*

DEVELOPMENTAL LEVEL
2–4

GROUP SIZE
Small

KEY EXPERIENCES

- *Measuring, testing, and analyzing: assessing the properties and composition of materials*

- *Observing, predicting, and controlling change: understanding causality*

- *Designing, building, fabricating, and modifying structures or materials*

- *Reporting and interpreting data and results*

—— A NOTE FOR TEACHERS ——

Energy Sources and Wind Power

The sun is our primary source of energy, and many of the secondary sources are easily and directly linked to it. The secondary sources of energy that are commonly known about are fossil fuels, water power, wind power, tidal energy, and nuclear energy. Less well-known sources include geothermal energy, fuel cell energy, and hydrogen gas, if it could be cheaply produced. Two major problems face the world in connection with its energy supply: the depletion of reserves and environmental pollution. Using power from the wind avoids both of these problems.

When children start investigating wind power the most likely question to arise is: What causes the wind to blow? Children will not be able to find the answer to this question directly or without help, but they can come close through their own observations and experiments. Wind is air moving across the Earth's surface. It is caused by the uneven heating of the atmosphere by the sun. Just like the air over a hot radiator or stove, air heated by the sun expands and rises. Cooler air from the Earth's surface flows in to take the place of the heated air. This process is called *circulation* and produces the flow of winds.

There are two types of circulation. A general one extends around the world. A secondary one produces local winds—winds that occur in only one place and in a limited area. Winds are named according to the direction from which they blow. Westerly winds blow from west to east, while a north wind blows from north to south. Young children can observe and record weather phenomena connected with wind direction and speed. Older children in the elementary school can set up and operate quite sophisticated weather stations, comparing their results and forecasts with those of the professional forecasters on television and radio.

Wind power can be used to turn a windmill blade, which can then be connected to simple machinery. Students can make two model windmill systems and compare their performance.

The first type is called a *twin-blade windmill* (see Illustration 10 on pg. 35). Students can make this type of windmill by following these steps.

- Use a cane or stick as a holder.

- Take a cork and cut a slit on either side of it at an angle.

- Into the slits glue two thin cardboard blades.

- Make a small hole in the cane through which a large pin can pass through easily.

- Push the pin through the hole and put a small bead on the pin.

- Continue pushing the pin through the hole and into the center of the cork.

• Once the twin-blade windmill is made, students can test it outdoors.

• Encourage them to experiment with different sizes of blades and angles of placing the blades in the cork. Note which works best.

The second type of windmill is a *pinwheel windmill* (see Illustration 11). This can be made with stiff paper as follows:

• Using stiff paper, 6" (15 cm) square, cut the pinwheel blades. Cut along the diagonals to make four triangles, leaving a small square uncut area in the center to keep the triangles attached. Then fold the lower right-hand corner of each triangle toward the center to make the pinwheel blades.

• Push a hole in the center so that the blade turns easily on a large pin.

• Take out the pin, put a bead on it, and push the bead up to the pinhead.

• Push the pin through the center hole of the blades, put on another bead, and then push the pin firmly into the cane.

• Test the windmill outdoors.

Have the students record the results of their tests and pose the following questions to students for discussion:

• Which windmill design uses the wind energy best?

• Can the designs be improved by alternating the size or shape of the blades or rotor?

• Which design works best in lighter winds?

• Which design works best in stronger winds?

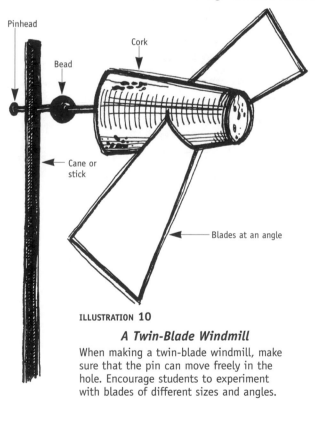

ILLUSTRATION 10

A Twin-Blade Windmill

When making a twin-blade windmill, make sure that the pin can move freely in the hole. Encourage students to experiment with blades of different sizes and angles.

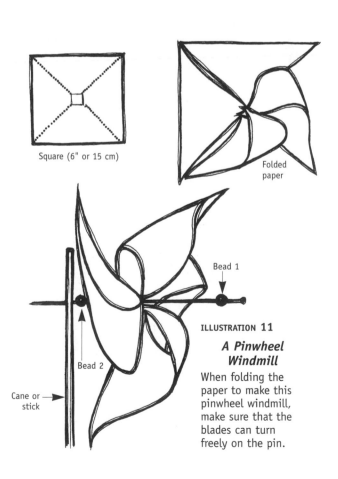

ILLUSTRATION 11

A Pinwheel Windmill

When folding the paper to make this pinwheel windmill, make sure that the blades can turn freely on the pin.

Energy and Wind Speeds ► *Activity 16*

DEVELOPMENTAL LEVEL
2–4

GROUP SIZE
Large

KEY EXPERIENCES

- *Measuring, testing, and analyzing: assessing the properties and composition of materials*

- *Observing, predicting, and controlling change: understanding causality*

- *Designing, building, fabricating, and modifying structures or materials*

- *Reporting and interpreting data and results*

One way students can estimate the strength of the wind is to go outside and feel the wind blowing on their faces. Another way is to observe the movements of trees. A better way than either of these is to have some standard method of measuring or estimating wind speed. An instrument that measures wind speed is called an anemometer. Students can create several, simple types of anemometers, such as the one shown in Illustration 12.

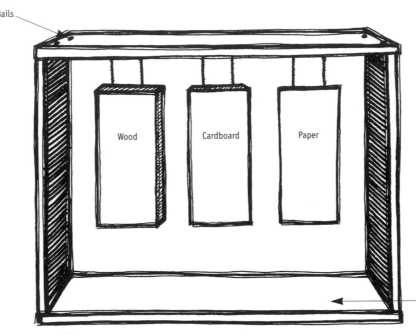

Nails

Wood   Cardboard   Paper

Wooden base

ILLUSTRATION 12

A Simple Anemometer for Outdoor Use

Students can make a simple anemometer by hanging a piece of wood, cardboard, and paper from a wooden framework. The speed of the wind can then be observed by watching the movement of these three items.

The simplest anemometer can be made by suspending within a frame pieces of three different materials, each of a different weight but of identical size, and holding this device in the wind. Students can make this type of anemometer by hanging a piece of wood, a piece of cardboard, and a piece of paper—all of identical size—from a wooden framework. They can attach the materials to the frame using short strings and cellophane tape. The device can be set next to an open window or taken outdoors and the movement of the materials observed.

- If all three materials are still, the wind is calm.

- If only the paper moves, there is a breeze.

- If the cardboard also moves, there is a light wind.

- If the wood blows as well, there is a strong wind.

Students should record the wind speed twice a day using a simple numbering system, such as calm = 1, breeze = 2, light wind = 3, and strong wind = 4. They can make a block graph of the wind force measured this way over the course a month.

A Simple Indoor Anemometer ► *Activity 17*

DEVELOPMENTAL LEVEL
2–4

GROUP SIZE
Small

KEY EXPERIENCES

• *Measuring, testing, and analyzing: assessing the properties and composition of materials*

• *Observing, predicting, and controlling change: understanding causality*

• *Designing, building, fabricating, and modifying structures or materials*

  • *Reporting and interpreting data and results*

When we can feel the movement of air indoors, we call it a draft. Students can make a more sensitive anemometer to detect air movement indoors (see Illustration 13).

Using a design similar to the outdoor anemometer, students can make an indoor device using a dry leaf, tissue paper, and a feather. These can be fixed to the frame with string and cellophane tape. Students can try the anemometer in various parts of the room and the school. As before, they can devise a simple scale to record the results. For example, they can use this range: still air (nothing moves) = 1; faintly moving air (only the dry leaf moves) = 2; moving air (tissue paper also moves) = 3; and draft (all three materials move) = 4. Students can draw plans of the room and the school on graph paper and show the air flow as measured on this apparatus. They can investigate the effect of opening and shutting doors and windows and record these results.

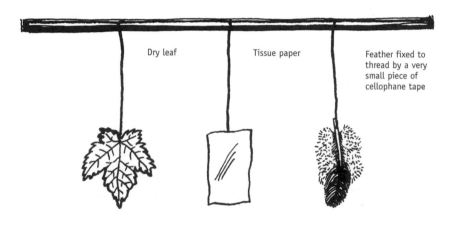

Dry leaf   Tissue paper   Feather fixed to thread by a very small piece of cellophane tape

ILLUSTRATION 13

A Simple Anemometer for Indoor Use

Using a dry leaf, tissue paper, and a feather, students can make a more sensitive anemometer to detect air movement indoors.

A More Advanced Anemometer ▶ *Activity 18*

DEVELOPMENTAL LEVEL
4–6

GROUP SIZE
Small

KEY EXPERIENCES

- *Measuring, testing, and analyzing: assessing the properties and composition of materials*
- *Observing, predicting, and controlling change: understanding causality*
- *Designing, building, fabricating, and modifying structures or materials*
- *Reporting and interpreting data and results*

Students can make a more sophisticated anemometer by following these steps (see Illustration 14).

- Cut two table tennis (Ping-Pong) balls in half. [**Note:** The teacher should do this.]

- Paint one half-ball red or black so that it can be seen easily.

- Make a hole in the center of a large cork, big enough to push in the plastic top from a ballpoint pen.

- Push wooden toothpicks into each half of the table tennis balls and put the free ends into the cork.

- Let the unit holding the half-balls turn on a sharp knitting needle or long pointed nail.

- Stick the free end of the knitting needle into a large lump of clay in a tin lid as a base.

- If the anemometer is working well, the cups should turn when they are blown on gently.

Students can test the air currents in the room under various conditions—by an open window, at the door when it is wide open, at the door when it is almost closed. They can also test the speed of the wind outdoors. Students can record the results, noting the speed of the moving cups. In a 5-step rating system, for example, the cups might move very slowly, slowly, medium, fast, and very fast. Next, the students can try to get more accurate results by counting the number of turns made by the colored cup in a minute. Have them keep records of the results of their wind-speed tests for several days or weeks. Discuss the conditions indoors and outdoors that are related to different wind speeds.

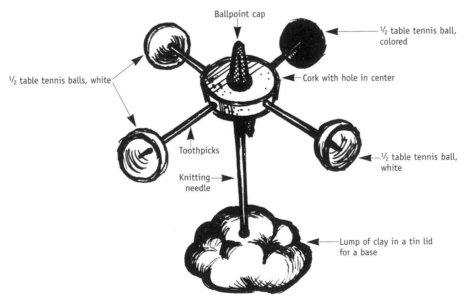

ILLUSTRATION 14

A More Sophisticated Anemometer
With a more elaborate anemometer, students can test air currents under various conditions—by an open window, in the school hallway, or at a door that is wide open.

Part Three

Human Energy

M ost activities in the world depend at some point on human energy. The first machines were aids to the application of human energy. Knives and forks, axes and spades, ladders and ropes—these are all simple aids that have enabled us to make great progress. Human energy can be transferred to simple machines quite easily. It can also be stored and then released gradually as it does its work.

Transfer of Human Energy ▶ *Activity 19*

DEVELOPMENTAL LEVEL
K–2

GROUP SIZE
Small

KEY EXPERIENCES

• *Measuring, testing, and analyzing: assessing the properties and composition of materials*

• *Observing, predicting, and controlling change: understanding causality*

• *Designing, building, fabricating, and modifying structures or materials*

Children will be well aware of human energy when they use the large-scale toys on a playground. Does the swing work on its own when you sit on it? What must be done to get it going if you are alone? How can it get going if you have a friend with you? How does the swing get its energy? (See Illustration 15.)

Will a bicycle go when you sit on it (see Illustration 16 on pg. 41)? What do you have to do to start it moving? What happens when you stop putting energy into the pedals? Whose energy causes the movement?

If there is a toy pedal car in the playground, how can this be powered by human energy? Can it be moved by other ways than pedaling? Can this be done alone or does the driver need a friend?

The following activity will help children explore how human energy is used and transferred. To begin, have students get the top of a circular container made of cardboard or thin plastic, about 3" (8 cm) in diameter, and stick plain paper on either side of the disk so that it can be colored. Let them divide the circle into four equal parts and color each part, using red, blue, yellow, and green. They should make two holes about 1" (2 cm) on either side of the center of the circle and thread thin, strong string through the holes. Pull the string through the holes and tie it to form two loops about 6" (15 cm) on each side of the disk. Have them give the disk a few turns and then pull on the loops to make the disk spin. Let them try this several times to get the rhythm of the pulls to transfer human energy to the energy of motion as the disk turns (see Illustration 17 on pg. 41).

The students can experiment with different patterns on the disks in different sizes. For example, they can try dividing the disk into six parts that are colored red,

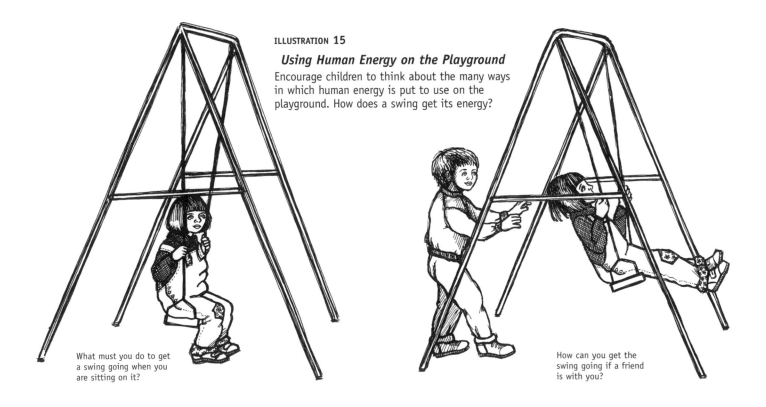

ILLUSTRATION **15**

Using Human Energy on the Playground

Encourage children to think about the many ways in which human energy is put to use on the playground. How does a swing get its energy?

What must you do to get a swing going when you are sitting on it?

How can you get the swing going if a friend is with you?

ILLUSTRATION **16**

Using Human Energy to Ride a Bike

Encourage children to think about the human energy needed to pedal a bike. What do you have to do to get the bike moving?

orange, yellow, green, blue, and indigo (purple)—the colors of the rainbow. Have them observe the resulting color when the disk turns.

After students get the disk turning very fast, have them listen carefully to see if any human energy is being turned into sound energy to make a noise. Next, have them make a few tooth-shaped cuts in the edge of the disk. Does this increase the sound? Let them experiment with different shaped cuts in the edge. Discuss the findings, comparing the results of the students' experiments with colors and cuts.

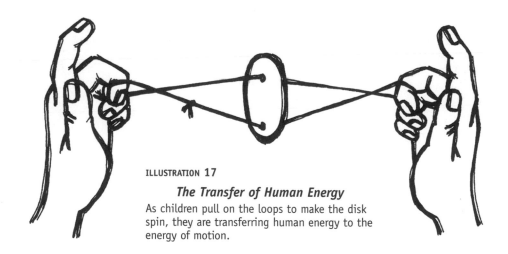

ILLUSTRATION **17**

The Transfer of Human Energy

As children pull on the loops to make the disk spin, they are transferring human energy to the energy of motion.

Transfer of Human Energy ► *Activity 20*

DEVELOPMENTAL LEVEL
1–3

GROUP SIZE
Small

KEY EXPERIENCES

- *Measuring, testing, and analyzing: assessing the properties and composition of materials*

- *Observing, predicting, and controlling change: understanding causality*

- *Designing, building, fabricating, and modifying structures or materials*

- *Reporting and interpreting data and results*

Get some toy "push and go" cars of exactly the same size and make. The cars should be numbered or have different colors for easy identification. Have students mark out a track on a small area of the floor with a starting line for the cars (see Illustration 18). Human energy can be put into them by pushing them firmly on the ground and then setting them down quickly at the starting line. Have students measure how far each car travels on its charge of energy and record the results. They should repeat the experiment several times to try to get the best result. Discuss the results and pose the following questions:

- How is the energy provided?

- Why do some cars do better than others?

- What factors cause energy loss?

- Why do the cars always stop?

Follow up the above experiments with similar ones using wind-up (spring-driven) cars. Have students record their results as before and discuss their findings.

- What are the differences between the types of cars? What advantages do spring-driven cars have over "push and go" cars?

- How does the energy get into the car spring?

- Why do some cars do better than others? How can you improve their performance?

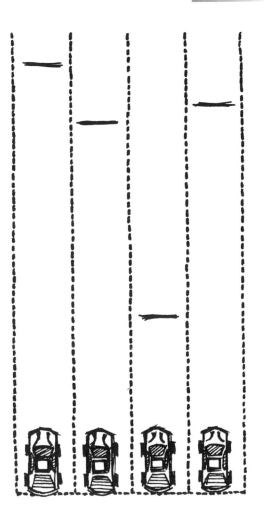

ILLUSTRATION 18

Observing the Transfer of Energy in Toy Cars

As children experiment with toy cars, encourage them to think about the following types of questions: Why do some cars travel farther than others? Why do the cars always stop? What factors cause energy loss?

Storing Human Energy ▶ *Activity 21*

DEVELOPMENTAL LEVEL
2–4

GROUP SIZE
Small

KEY EXPERIENCES

• *Measuring, testing, and analyzing: assessing the properties and composition of materials*

• *Observing, predicting, and controlling change: understanding causality*

• *Designing, building, fabricating, and modifying structures or materials*

• *Reporting and interpreting data and results*

One way to store energy is to put it into springs or similar materials. Elastic bands can be used in this way. The following spool tractor, made from an empty thread spool, stores energy and then puts that energy to use.

Students can make this type of tractor from an empty thread spool, an elastic band, a toothpick, a piece of candle, and a thumbtack (see Illustration 19). Rub the candle wax along the outside rims of the spool (the tractor "tires") to make it roll smoothly. Slide the elastic band through the center of the spool. Anchor the elastic band at one end of the spool with a thumbtack. Slip the toothpick through the opening in the elastic band. Then set down the spool tractor and let it go.

Winding up the elastic band will give the tractor energy. Students can test its performance after giving the elastic different numbers of turns (different amounts of power). Have them record the results and pose the following questions and activities for discussion:

• Is there a limit to the usable power?

• Try putting on rubber bands as tires. Does this improve the performance?

• What is the steepest slope it will climb?

• What happens when it is on a very smooth surface? A rough surface? What surface gives the best performance?

Students can try tractors made from spools of different sizes. Have them make performance charts to compare the results for the different models over different courses and obstacles.

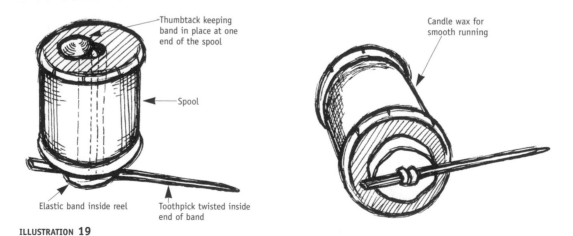

Thumbtack keeping band in place at one end of the spool

Spool

Elastic band inside reel

Toothpick twisted inside end of band

Candle wax for smooth running

ILLUSTRATION 19

A Spool Tractor

Students can make a simple tractor from a spool of thread, an elastic band, a toothpick, a piece of candle, and a thumbtack. Winding up the elastic band gives the tractor its energy.

Storing Human Energy ▶ *Activity 22*

DEVELOPMENTAL LEVEL
3–5

GROUP SIZE
Small

KEY EXPERIENCES

- *Measuring, testing, and analyzing: assessing the properties and composition of materials*

- *Observing, predicting, and controlling change: understanding causality*

- *Designing, building, fabricating, and modifying structures or materials*

- *Reporting and interpreting data and results*

Another type of device that stores and uses energy is the giant bull-dozer tractor, which students can make from a plastic squeeze bottle. The drive is from two large elastic bands linked together. The bottom of the bottle is pierced to allow the elastic to be pulled through and attached to a nail, held in place with two large staples. The wire can come from an old coat hanger. It is bent into a hook shape to go into the bottle and to pick up the elastic. Then the top of the bottle is threaded over the wire and the nozzle hole is opened so that the wire runs freely through the hole. The wire is bent at right angles to the bottle and its free end is fixed to a plate of stiff cardboard (see Illustration 20). Cellophane tape or another large staple can be used for this.

Have students test the bulldozer tractor in the same way as the spool tractor and compare the results. Let them devise some special hill-climbing tests and investigate the results of putting tires on the tractor. They can record the results in block graphs and in figures.

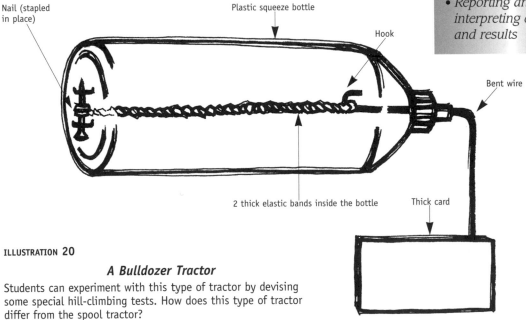

Nail (stapled in place)

Plastic squeeze bottle

Hook

Bent wire

2 thick elastic bands inside the bottle

Thick card

ILLUSTRATION 20

A Bulldozer Tractor

Students can experiment with this type of tractor by devising some special hill-climbing tests. How does this type of tractor differ from the spool tractor?

Part Four

Sound Energy

S ound is all around us. Absolute silence is never experienced in ordinary living conditions. All sounds have one thing in common—they are produced by vibrations. These vibrations are called "sound waves." A source of energy is needed to produce the vibrations. This source can be as varied as the power of the human voice, the notes of musical instruments, the noise of engines, and the roar of the waves.

Sound

Sound is produced when longitudinal waves travel along the back-and-forth movement of a vibrating object. This movement in turn moves the surrounding air, first compressing it and then allowing it to expand behind the compression. These compressions and expansions near the source of the sound also compress and expand the air further away until the energy weakens so much that the movement ceases. Sound requires a medium in which to travel. In many cases it is air, but any substance (solid, liquid, or gas) will do. Where there is no medium, sound cannot travel. Hence, a bell put into a vacuum jar cannot be heard even though its clapper can be seen vibrating.

The speed of sound in air was first measured in the early seventeenth century by observing the time between seeing the flash of a gun and hearing its sound. A simple calculation of the speed of sound can be made during the interval between seeing lightning and hearing the thunder. At normal temperatures the lightning will be about 1 mile away for every 5 seconds between the flash and the thunder. (This is about 1 kilometer for every 3 seconds.) In the air, sound travels 1,100 feet (335 meters) per second. Sound travels through water at 4,700 feet (1,430 meters) per second, through brick at 11,900 feet (3,624 meters) per second, and through steel at 16,400 feet (5,000 meters) per second.

The ear is constructed to catch sound waves that come to it through the air. Sound waves enter the tubes from the outer ear to the eardrum and cause it to vibrate. These vibrations are transmitted via special nerves to the brain, which interprets what is heard. If a sound does not have enough energy in its vibrations to make the eardrums vibrate, the sound is said to be inaudible. The energy content of sound is really very small. If all the energy of normal speech could be converted into heat it would take 1,000,000 people talking for one and a half hours to make a cup of hot tea. The power of 10,000 people cheering at their loudest would only produce enough energy to light an ordinary electric lamp.

A Speaking Tube ▶ *Activity 23*

DEVELOPMENTAL LEVEL
K–2

GROUP SIZE
Small

KEY EXPERIENCES

• *Measuring, testing, and analyzing: assessing the properties and composition of materials*

• *Designing, building, fabricating, and modifying structures or materials*

• *Reporting and interpreting data and results*

In this activity, students make a simple telephone. To begin, have them get a length of garden hose (about 6 yards or 6 meters) and put a funnel into each end of the hose so that it fits tightly. Working in pairs, one child stays in the room and holds the funnel to his or her ear while the other takes the hose through the doorway and as far out of the room as it will stretch. The children take turns whispering messages to each other (see Illustration 21). The receiver should repeat the message to the sender, who acknowledges whether it was correctly received (repeating it if need be); then the children change roles.

Students can test the telephone in several ways. Does it work around corners? Does it work from low levels to higher levels (from downstairs to upstairs)? Does it work if a cork is placed in one end or in both ends? Can music be heard through it (for example, a transistor radio playing softly or a harmonica)?

ILLUSTRATION 21

Creating a Speaking Tube
After making a simple telephone, children can investigate many properties of sound.

─── A NOTE FOR TEACHERS ───

The Energy of Various Sources of Sound

The energy produced by speech organs sets air moving, and this air carries the sound along. The louder the sound, the more energy is needed to produce it. This is evident when playing a musical instrument. When the air movement is prevented, the sound is stopped. Sound involves the conversion of one type of energy into another, for example, wind energy into sound energy when blowing a trumpet. Mechanical conversions of one type of energy into sound energy include hand clapping and hammering. Chemical conversions include explosions, and electrical conversions produce the sound heard on radios and cassette players.

Investigating Sound Energy: Making a Stethoscope ▶ *Activity 24*

DEVELOPMENTAL LEVEL
1–3

GROUP SIZE
Small

KEY EXPERIENCES

• *Measuring, testing, and analyzing: assessing the properties and composition of materials*

• *Observing, predicting, and controlling change: understanding causality*

• *Designing, building, fabricating, and modifying structures or materials*

• *Reporting and interpreting data and results*

Sound energy can be investigated by making a simple stethoscope constructed with a small, hollow plastic tube (narrower than a garden hose) and smaller funnels for the ends (see Illustration 22). Have students cut the tops from two empty squeeze bottles to provide listening cups. The two cups should be put on either end of about 30" (50 cm) of plastic tubing. It may be necessary to bind or pack the ends of the tube to get a good fit into the ear cups.

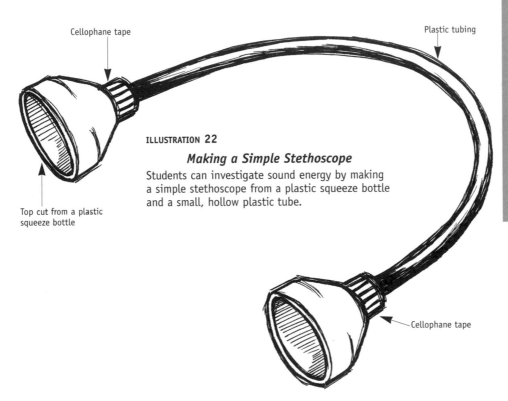

Cellophane tape

Plastic tubing

Top cut from a plastic squeeze bottle

Cellophane tape

ILLUSTRATION 22

Making a Simple Stethoscope

Students can investigate sound energy by making a simple stethoscope from a plastic squeeze bottle and a small, hollow plastic tube.

Put a wind-up watch (not an electronic one) on the table. Have students place one end of the stethoscope over the watch and listen to the other end. How clearly can they hear the watch? Do they hear better with or without the stethoscope? Next, have students put one end of the stethoscope on their chest (this works best if they are wearing thin shirts) and listen to the other end. Can they hear their hearts beating? Have them first listen to their heartbeat when they are sitting quietly. Next, have them go outside and run around the playground until they are breathing rapidly and then listen to their heartbeat again. What changes are there? Let the students think up other activities and listen to their heartbeats after each one. Discuss the results.

Students can also make a more sophisticated stethoscope that lets them listen with both ears (see Illustration 23 on pg. 49). Using thin plastic tubing, a T-shaped piece of metal or plastic (obtainable at a hardware store), and a small funnel cut from the top of a plastic bottle, students can construct a stethoscope that looks quite similar to the kind used by doctors. Let students repeat the ticking watch and heartbeat experiments and compare how well they can hear with the two types of stethoscopes.

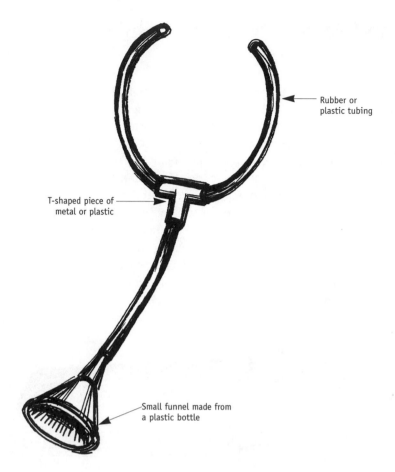

Rubber or
plastic tubing

T-shaped piece of
metal or plastic

Small funnel made from
a plastic bottle

ILLUSTRATION 23

Making a More Sophisticated Stethoscope

Using thin plastic tubing, a T-shaped piece of metal or plastic, and a small funnel, students can make a stethoscope that looks similar to the kind used by doctors.

Feeling Sound Energy ▶ *Activity 25*

DEVELOPMENTAL LEVEL
2–4

GROUP SIZE
Large

KEY EXPERIENCES

- *Measuring, testing, and analyzing: assessing the properties and composition of materials*

- *Observing, predicting, and controlling change: understanding causality*

- *Designing, building, fabricating, and modifying structures or materials*

- *Reporting and interpreting data and results*

Students can feel the energy that sounds produce with the following simple apparatus. Begin with a large strong cardboard tube or tin can at least 4" (10 cm) across, with both the ends removed. Have students tightly stretch a large piece of rubber from a balloon over one end of the tube and keep it in place with cellophane tape, a strong elastic band, or string tightly tied around it. Leave the other end of the tube open (see Illustration 24). Working in pairs, have one student clap twice near the open end of the tube while another student holds the tube and very gently touches the rubber with his or her fingertips. Can anything be felt in response to the sound? Have students repeat this investigation with loud speech and soft speech. They can also try the effect of musical instruments played near the open end of the tube. Have them think of other sounds to try.

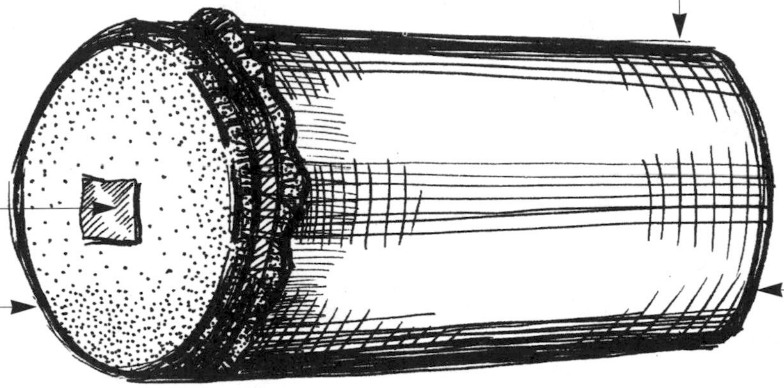

Strong cardboard tube

Shiny metal foil

Balloon rubber stretched tightly over the end and held in place

Open end 4" to 6" in diameter (10 cm)

ILLUSTRATION 24

A Sound Detector

As students experiment with different sources of sound (the human voice, musical instruments, tools), encourage them to think about the source of the energy that causes the rubber to vibrate.

Next have students stick a piece of shiny metal foil, about ½" (1 cm) square, in the center of the rubber. Let sunlight or the light from a lamp shine on the square so that it reflects on a wall. Have students speak, sing, and make various noises into the open end of the tube. What happens to the spot of reflected light? When a musical instrument is played into the tube, does the light respond more to some notes than others? What effect does changing the distance of the source of the sound from the open end of the tube have on the amount of vibration? As students try different sources of sounds—the human voice, instruments, hand tools, and so on—discuss where the energy comes from that causes the rubber to vibrate.

How Sound Travels ▶ *Activity 26*

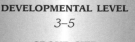

DEVELOPMENTAL LEVEL
3–5

GROUP SIZE
Small

KEY EXPERIENCES

- *Measuring, testing, and analyzing: assessing the properties and composition of materials*

- *Observing, predicting, and controlling change: understanding causality*

- *Designing, building, fabricating, and modifying structures or materials*

- *Reporting and interpreting data and results*

The activities presented so far in this section have explored the energy produced by sound traveling through the air. The following activity illustrates that sound also travels well through solids and liquids. To begin, put a spring-wound clock or watch at one end of a table. Have students put an ear to the other end of the table and listen to the ticking. Does the sound travel best through the table or the air? Put the watch on the floor and carefully rest a 3' (1 meter) ruler or length of wood on it. Have students listen at the other end of the wood. Is the sound louder or softer than through the air?

Next have students try listening through another solid medium—wood. Using a wooden stick about the length of their arms, students should put one end of the stick on a ticking watch and the other end in their mouths (see Illustration 25). (**Note:** Make sure the stick is thoroughly washed before and after each use.) Then they should put cotton plugs (or earplugs, as used in swimming) in their ears so that the sound cannot travel through the air to their eardrums. Now, can they hear the watch? How does the sound get to them? Have them think about all the places the sound moves through in this experiment.

Students can also make a string telephone (see Illustration 26). Have them try plastic cups, waxed cartons, and cans as earpieces to see which works best. The string must always be taut when sending messages, and it must not touch any object that is between the earpieces. What is the greatest length they can have for the string when speaking? What is the greatest length when sending messages by tapping or plucking the string? Does thin wire or nylon fishing line work as well as string?

ILLUSTRATION 25

Investigating How Sound Travels

In this experiment, students explore how sound travels through a solid medium, such as wood. With their ears plugged, can they hear the ticking of the watch? How does the sound get to them?

ILLUSTRATION 26

A String Telephone

Working in pairs, students take turns speaking and then listening through a string telephone.

Spoon Chimes ► *Activity 27*

DEVELOPMENTAL LEVEL
1–3

GROUP SIZE
Small

KEY EXPERIENCES

• *Measuring, testing, and analyzing: assessing the properties and composition of materials*

• *Observing, predicting, and controlling change: understanding causality*

• *Designing, building, fabricating, and modifying structures or materials*

• *Reporting and interpreting data and results*

Students can make simple spoon chimes by tying several metal spoons to the end of a piece of string so that they rattle together when shaken. With a finger, have them hold the free end of the string firmly to their ear and shake the spoons. What do they hear? How can they explain what happens? Now have them join two strings to the spoons so that one goes to each of their ears. What difference does it make? Let them try other items in addition to the spoons on the end of the strings. (See Illustration 27.)

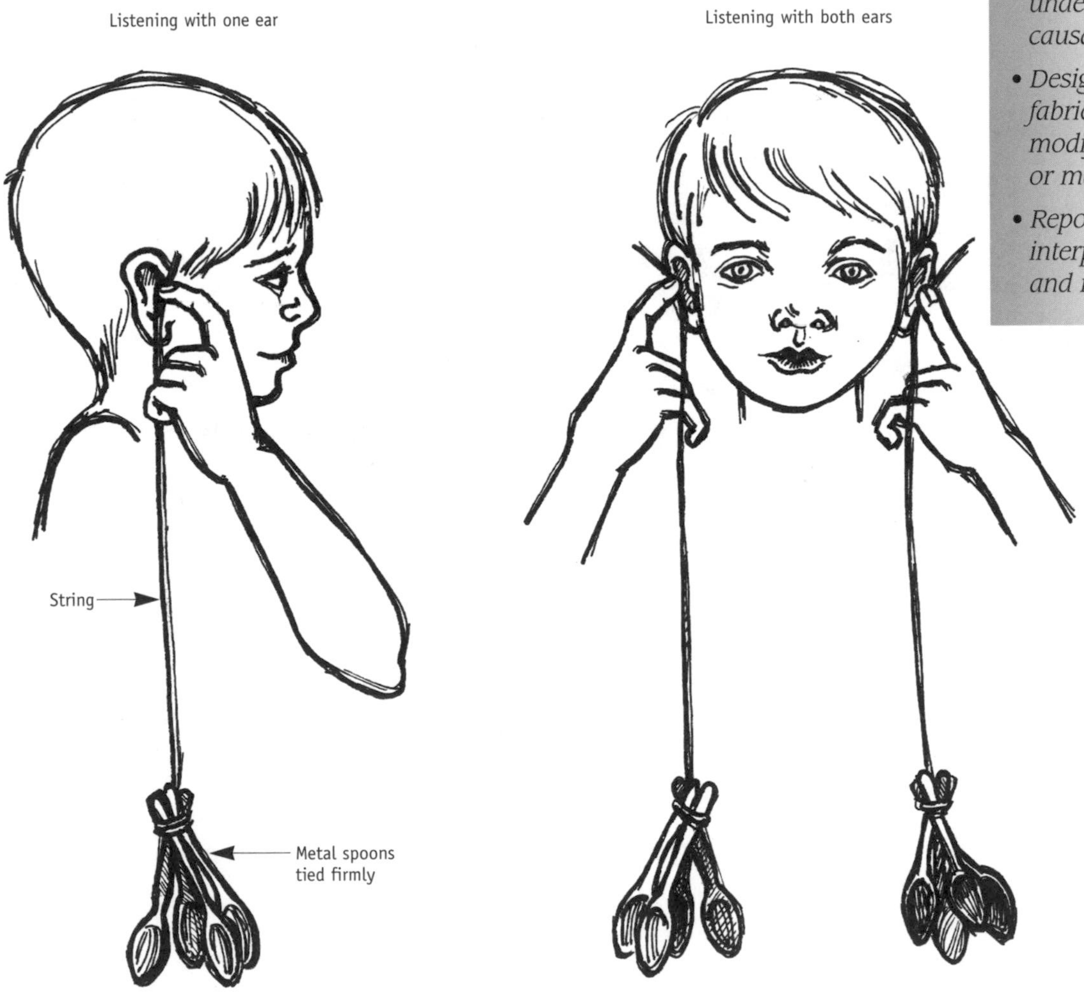

Listening with one ear

Listening with both ears

String →

← Metal spoons tied firmly

ILLUSTRATION 27

Spoon Chimes

After making simple spoon chimes, students can hold the free end of the string to their ears and shake the spoons. What do they hear? Next, they join two strings to the spoons and listen with both ears.

Making Musical Instruments ▶ *Activity 28*

DEVELOPMENTAL LEVEL
4–6

GROUP SIZE
Small

KEY EXPERIENCES

• *Measuring, testing, and analyzing: assessing the properties and composition of materials*

• *Observing, predicting, and controlling change: understanding causality*

• *Designing, building, fabricating, and modifying structures or materials*

• *Reporting and interpreting data and results*

One interesting way for students to explore sound energy is by examining real and toy musical instruments—trumpets, guitars, violins, drums, saxophones, and so on. Pose the following questions:

• What is vibrating to cause the sound in each instrument?

• How is it made to vibrate?

• How is the note changed?

• How many notes can it make? A few or many?

Students can also make their own musical instruments. Here is how they can make *bottle bells* (see Illustration 28).

• Get eight glass bottles of the same size.

• Leave one bottle empty and put different amounts of water in the other bottles.

• First tap the empty bottle. What is vibrating to make the sound?

• Now tap each of the other bottles gently. What do you notice about the sound and the amount of water in each? What is vibrating to make the sound when you tap a bottle?

ILLUSTRATION **28**

Bottle Bells

Students can make bottle bells from eight empty glass bottles of the same size. Have them fill seven of the bottles with different amounts of water and leave one bottle empty. After gently tapping each bottle, what do the students notice about the relationship between the sound made and the amount of water in a bottle?

• Tune the bottles by adding more water and try to get a scale.

Next, students can make a *rubber-band band* (see Illustration 29 on pg. 54). To begin, let them stretch different widths of rubber bands around an open box as a base (for example, a rectangular plastic tub or the top or bottom half of a cardboard box). They should use at least four different widths of rubber bands. The box acts as a sounding board and makes the sound louder. As they pluck each band, have students listen to the note it makes. How does the width of the band affect the sound it makes? What difference does the tension (tightness) of the band make?

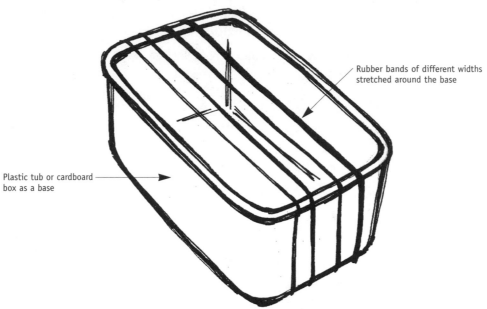

Rubber bands of different widths stretched around the base

Plastic tub or cardboard box as a base

ILLUSTRATION 29

A Rubber-band Instrument

As they pluck each band and listen to the sound produced, encourage students to think about how the width and the tautness of the rubber bands affect the sound.

Part Five

Heat Energy

Heat is an important type of energy. It warms our homes, runs the machinery that is essential to the production of electrical energy, and performs a vital function in the bodies of all warm-bodied animals, including humans.

Heat Energy

We often react to the concept of "heat" in a subjective way: We think of how heat makes us *feel.* But the question "What is heat?" has fascinated people ever since fire was discovered and used as a source of heat. In the seventeenth century, Galileo's thermoscope (a device that measured variations in temperature without measuring the actual amount) was the first of the modern developments in the study of heat. Back then, people still thought of heat as a substance. Prior to the middle of the eighteenth century, the words *heat, temperature,* and *fire* all meant the same thing. Later, heat was considered to be a type of fluid that influenced the bodies it entered. Confusion about the nature of heat continued until the middle of the nineteenth century. There were two schools of thought at that time—the "calorists" who thought heat was a weightless fluid, and the "new thinkers," who contended that heat had something to do with molecular agitation. The latter thinking paved the way for the present understanding of heat as a form of energy.

All things are made up of constantly moving atoms and molecules. Their motion gives objects an internal energy. The level of this energy depends on how quickly the particles move. If they move slowly, the object has a low level of internal energy; if they move rapidly, the object has a high level of internal energy. Hot objects have a higher level of internal energy than cold objects. We refer to this as the "temperature" of an object.

Heat passes from one object or place to another by three means—conduction, convection, and radiation. *Conduction* is the movement of heat through a material without carrying any material with it. The atoms in the hot part vibrate faster, strike adjoining atoms, and increase the movement of atoms throughout all of the material. *Convection* is the transfer of heat by the movement of the heated material itself. Thus, hot air rises and is replaced by cooler air, and this movement is called a "convection current." Convection occurs in liquids as well as gases. In both conduction and convection the moving particles transmit heat energy. But heat can also travel through empty space because in any object the moving particles create infrared waves of radiant energy. Hot objects give off more infrared rays than cold ones. When this radiant energy strikes an object, it speeds up the movement of the object's atoms or molecules and the object becomes warmer; this process is known as *radiation.* Much of the energy from the sun travels through space to the earth. It is these rays which warm us, the atmosphere, the seas, and the surface of the Earth itself.

Heat Energy From the Sun ▶ *Activity 29*

DEVELOPMENTAL LEVEL
2–4

GROUP SIZE
Small

KEY EXPERIENCES

• *Measuring, testing, and analyzing: assessing the properties and composition of materials*

• *Observing, predicting, and controlling change: understanding causality*

• *Designing, building, fabricating, and modifying structures or materials*

• *Reporting and interpreting data and results*

We can all feel the heat energy from the sun merely by walking from the shade to the sun. Heat energy from the sun can be concentrated by using a magnifying glass. Here is an experiment for students to set up. (See Illustration 30.)

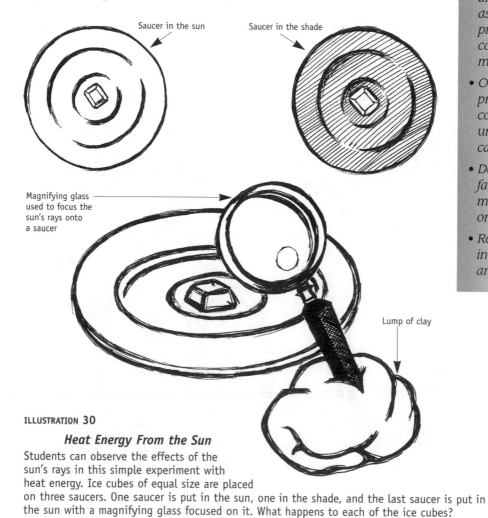

Saucer in the sun

Saucer in the shade

Magnifying glass used to focus the sun's rays onto a saucer

Lump of clay

ILLUSTRATION 30

Heat Energy From the Sun

Students can observe the effects of the sun's rays in this simple experiment with heat energy. Ice cubes of equal size are placed on three saucers. One saucer is put in the sun, one in the shade, and the last saucer is put in the sun with a magnifying glass focused on it. What happens to each of the ice cubes?

• Get three saucers.

• In each saucer, put an ice cube. Make sure they are cubes of equal size.

• Put one saucer in the shade.

• Put the second saucer in the sun.

• Put the third saucer in the sun with a magnifying glass focused on it. In this condition, the ice cube is getting both the direct rays of the sun and the reflected rays of the sun. Stick the handle of the magnifying glass into a large lump of clay to act as a firm base. (If necessary, extend the handle by tying on extra sticks.) Position the magnifying glass to focus the sun's rays on the ice cube. The rays are at their strongest when the point of light is at its smallest.

Have students make a note of the time when the experiment started and then watch each saucer to see when the ice cube is entirely melted into water. Have them note when each ice cube melted completely under each condition and set these results out in a table showing starting time, melting time, and total time for the melting.

The sun's heat energy can also be concentrated by mirrors (see Illustration 31). Have students set up the three saucers and ice cubes as before—one in the shade, one in the sun, and one in the sun with a reflector—but this time make the a reflector with hand mirrors. Use two or three mirrors set in lumps of clay. As with the magnifying glass, position the mirrors so that they reflect the sun's rays onto the ice cube. Which block of ice melted first? Which melted next? Which melted last? Discuss these results and elicit explanations for the differential rates of melting.

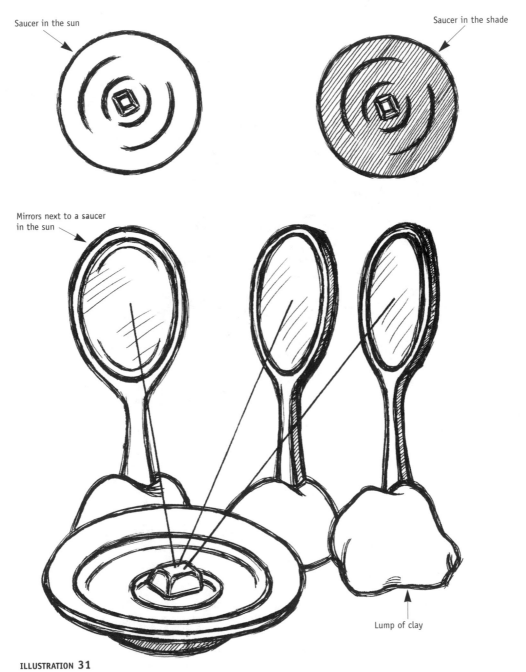

Saucer in the sun

Saucer in the shade

Mirrors next to a saucer in the sun

Lump of clay

ILLUSTRATION **31**

Concentrating the Sun's Heat Energy With Mirrors

The sun's heat energy can also be concentrated by small mirrors that are positioned to reflect the sun's rays onto an ice cube on a saucer.

Staying Warm: Keeping Heat Energy From Escaping ▶ *Activity 30*

DEVELOPMENTAL LEVEL
K–2

GROUP SIZE
Large

KEY EXPERIENCES

- *Measuring, testing, and analyzing: assessing the properties and composition of materials*

- *Observing, predicting, and controlling change: understanding causality*

- *Designing, building, fabricating, and modifying structures or materials*

- *Reporting and interpreting data and results*

___ A NOTE FOR TEACHERS ___

Insulation

"Insulation" is a method of controlling the movement of heat by keeping it in—or out—of a place. Houses are designed to keep heat in during winter and out during summer. The three ways by which heat is transferred form the basis for designing ways of dealing with unwanted heat transfer. Materials such as wood or plastic make good insulators against the transfer of heat by conduction. That is why they make good coverings for the handles of pots and pans. The utensil heats rapidly, but the handle stays cool where the conduction is poor. The movement of air by convection can be controlled by blocking the space between a hot and cold area with trapped or dead air. This is best seen in the air between inner and outer windows. Surfaces that reflect infrared rays can reduce heating by radiation. Thus, shiny metal roofs reflect the sun's rays away from the house. Conversely, heat can be collected by solar heating panels placed on the roof. The panels use the sun's heat to provide hot water. A look around the average house will give good examples of the ways that insulation is used in the home. A fiberglass blanket is spread in the attic, loose fill insulation is poured or blown into spaces between walls, rigid insulation boards are fixed to walls, and reflective covers are placed behind radiators.

These principles also operate in clothing. Wool clothes are warmer than those made of other fabrics. Air becomes trapped in the wool fibers. Because the fibers do not conduct heat rapidly, the wool forms a protective layer between the warmth of the body and the cold outside it. This keeps down heat loss from the body. Conversely, lightweight and light-colored clothes reflect the sun's rays away from the body and are cooler to wear in summer.

To test various forms of insulation, have students get four cans of the same size with lids. Empty soda pop cans work well for this. Have them prepare covers for the cans and lids as follows (see Illustration 32 on pg. 60).

- For the first can, cut out a piece of wool and fix it around the can with two elastic bands. Cut a cover to place over the lid.

- For the second can, begin by filling a large plastic bag with loose cotton wool; then place the can inside, making sure that the wool goes all around the sides, top, and bottom of the can.

- For the third can, cut an aluminum foil covering with the shiny side facing in to wrap around the outside and cut out a covering for the bottom and for the lid.

- Leave the fourth can as it is.

- Put hot—not boiling—water in each can. Replace the lids and coverings.

- Put all the cans in a row in a place where they will not be disturbed.

Can covered with a woolen cloth

Can surrounded by cotton wool and covered by a plastic bag

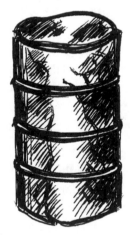

Can covered with aluminum foil, shiny side facing in

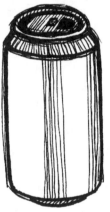

Uncovered can

ILLUSTRATION 32

Keeping in Heat

To test various forms of insulation, have students cover four cans with different types of materials. Pour hot water into each can, replace the cover, and feel the outside of each can. Which one is the warmest?

- After 5 minutes remove the covers and feel the outside of each can.

Pose the following questions for discussion: Which can feels warmest? Which is coolest? Have students continue the experiment as follows:

- Replace the covers.

- After 10 minutes, open the lids and carefully feel the temperature of the water in each can.

Pose the following questions again: Which can has the warmest water? Which has the coolest? Have students arrange the cans in order of warmest to coolest. Let them compare the temperature on the outside of the cans after five minutes and the temperature of the water inside the cans after ten minutes. Discuss what could have caused these differences.

Students can repeat this experiment using different materials to cover the cans. Make sure they first rinse the cans with cold water so that they all start at the same temperature. Other materials that students can use include plastic foam, paper, and polystyrene. Always leave the fourth can uncovered. Again, put hot water into the cans and feel the outside temperature after 5 minutes and the inside water temperature after 10 minutes. Compare these results with those of the previous experiment. Explore the implications for the various coverings concerning their ability to keep heat in (to insulate) and to let heat through (to transfer heat from one source to another). Discuss the problem of keeping warm in winter and cool in summer. What are the best materials for clothing at different times of year?

Heat Energy and Conduction of Heat ▶ *Activity 31*

DEVELOPMENTAL LEVEL
2–4

GROUP SIZE
Small

KEY EXPERIENCES

- *Measuring, testing, and analyzing: assessing the properties and composition of materials*

- *Observing, predicting, and controlling change: understanding causality*

- *Designing, building, fabricating, and modifying structures or materials*

- *Reporting and interpreting data and results*

Heat energy travels through some materials well and through others badly. To explore this concept, have students try the following two experiments.

First, have them get two metal spoons and two plastic spoons of the same size. Put them in cold water so that they will be at the same temperature. Fill a cup with hot (not boiling) water and put the spoons inside the cup. After 5 minutes feel each. What differences do you feel?

Second, use four 4" nails and a cup or basin shallow enough so that the upper half of the nails extends beyond the top. Leave one nail unwrapped as a control. Wrap the top half of one nail with adhesive tape, one with string, and one with the cap from a felt-tipped pen and packed with modeling clay (see Illustration 33). Fill the container with hot (not boiling) water. After five minutes, feel the top halves of the nails. Pose the following questions for discussion: Which covering would make the best handle for a kettle? Which covering would last the longest? Have students make a list of the types of handles used in kettles, saucepans, and other objects exposed to heat.

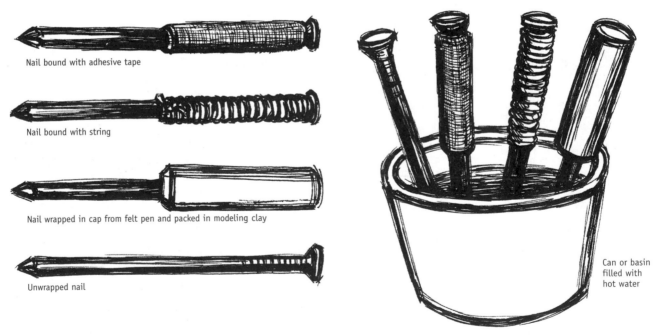

Nail bound with adhesive tape

Nail bound with string

Nail wrapped in cap from felt pen and packed in modeling clay

Unwrapped nail

Can or basin filled with hot water

ILLUSTRATION 33

Experimenting With Heat Conduction

Students can explore many simple properties of heat conduction in this experiment. Which covering would make the best handle for a kettle?

Heat Energy and Air ▶ *Activity 32*

DEVELOPMENTAL LEVEL
2–4

GROUP SIZE
Large

KEY EXPERIENCES

- *Measuring, testing, and analyzing: assessing the properties and composition of materials*

- *Observing, predicting, and controlling change: understanding causality*

- *Designing, building, fabricating, and modifying structures or materials*

- *Reporting and interpreting data and results*

The behavior of the air around us and its reaction to heat energy is an important influence in our lives. Students can see what happens to air when it gets hotter with a metal gallon can, a plastic bag, and a large bucket (see Illustration 34). First, help the students establish the fact that the can is filled with air. Ask them if the can is empty. Then have them put the can in a sink half full of water, immerse it, and observe bubbles coming out of the can as it fills with water. Explain that these are bubbles of air coming out. Let them fill the can completely with water. Have them reverse the process. As they empty the water out of the can, ask them what takes the place of the water inside the can. Help them understand that they now have a can full of air.

Next have the students flatten a plastic bag (make sure it is completely flat and contains no air) and attach it to the top of the can, sealing it tightly with cellophane tape and string. The air is now imprisoned in the can and it cannot get out; it is sealed inside.

Students should next fill a large bucket with hot (not boiling) water, push the can into the hot water as far as it will go, and keep it there. Have them watch what happens to the plastic bag. The heat energy from the hot water will be transferred to the air in the can. Ask them: What happens to the plastic bag? What causes the change?

When there is no further reaction, have students take the can out of the water, pour the hot water out of the bucket, and replace it with

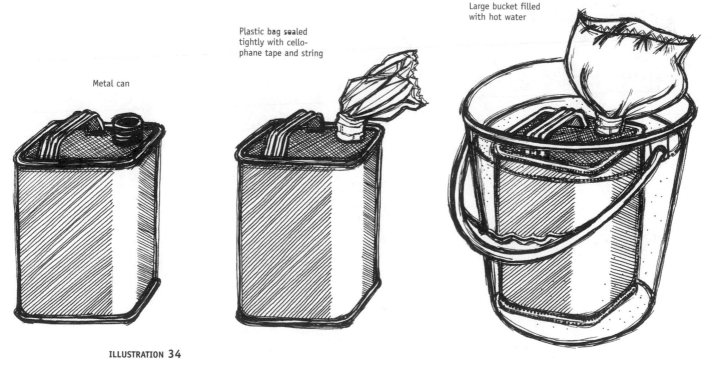

Metal can

Plastic bag sealed tightly with cello- phane tape and string

Large bucket filled with hot water

ILLUSTRATION **34**

Heat Energy and Air

Using a metal gallon can, a plastic bag, and a large bucket, students can observe how air reacts to heat energy. What happens to the plastic bag when the can is put in hot water? What causes the change?

cold water. Have one student hold the can down in the bucket while another adds more cold water. Again, have the students watch what happens to the plastic bag. Ask: What happens to the bag this time? What do you think causes this? Repeat this series of activities several times and have the students think about each stage:

• The can starts out with cold air inside and the flat plastic bag is sealed to its opening.

• The can with the flat plastic bag is put in the hot water. The heat energy from the water is transferred to the air in the can.

• What happens to the air? Does it try to get out of the can? If so, how does it do this? What does this do to the plastic bag?

• Why does another change happen when the can is put into the cold water?

Part Six

Weather

The weather changes constantly. One day it may be fine and sunny, the next cloudy and wet. Even on the same day, changes take place in the four main factors that make up the weather. These four elements are temperature, wind, moisture or humidity, and air pressure. Children can observe all of these features and make simple devices to measure or detect them as they explore "Energy and Change."

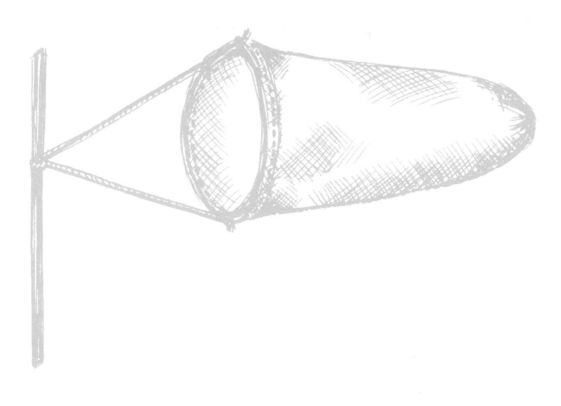

The Weather

The greatest influence on our weather is the sun. The sun sends enormous amounts of energy through space, some of which falls on this planet. The atmosphere traps sunshine rather like a greenhouse and it is in the atmosphere that weather systems arise.

It may be useful to define some of the common terms used in connection with the weather. "Air masses" are huge bodies of air having the same weather conditions throughout. A "front" is a long narrow band of changing weather between two kinds of air masses. "Lows" or "cyclones" are large areas of low pressure. Higher "anticyclones" are large areas of high pressure. "Wind" is the result of the movement of masses of air. "Temperature" is the measure of the degree of heat in the air. "Humidity" is the amount of water vapor or moisture in the air. When this moisture falls on Earth as rain, snow, hail, or sleet, we call it "precipitation." "Pressure" is the force produced by the weight of air pressing down on the Earth. Air generally moves from a high pressure area to a low pressure area. In the same way, winds blow out of the high to the low pressure areas.

There are many instruments for monitoring and measuring the weather. Temperature is measured with a thermometer, which has a scale graduated by degrees. The scale on a thermometer may be either Fahrenheit or Celsius (also called centigrade). The Fahrenheit scale has 180 divisions (degrees) between the freezing point of water (32°F) and the boiling point of water (212°F). The Celsius scale has 100 divisions between these two fixed points, with the freezing point at 0° C and the boiling point at 100°C. Wind speed is measured by an anemometer, and wind direction is measured by a weather vane. Pressure is measured by a barometer and is recorded in inches or millibars. A millibar is 1/1000 of a bar, which is a pressure of 29.53 inches of mercury at sea level. A mercury barometer is a long glass tube with one end sealed and the open end in a cup of mercury. As the air pressure changes, so does the height of the mercury in the tube. Many household barometers are in the form of an airtight box, the surfaces of which move as air pressure changes. These movements control a pointer on a dial that indicates the barometric pressure.

Weather Studies ▶ *Activity 33*

DEVELOPMENTAL LEVEL
K–2

GROUP SIZE
Large

KEY EXPERIENCES

• *Looking with a purpose: observing and collecting data*

• *Measuring, testing, and analyzing: assessing the properties and composition of materials*

• *Reporting and interpreting data and results*

Environmental change can be relatively rapid or imperceptibly slow. Young children will not stay with long-term studies of the more subtle changes, but they will certainly sustain activities concerning shorter-term changes. Begin weather studies by observing changes over a single day—the position of the sun, appearance of the sky, temperature, wind speed, and rainfall. Most of the equipment for these studies can be made by children in the classroom; only a thermometer needs to be purchased. Children can use their observational skills to describe the sky—sunny, mixture of clouds and sun, cloudy. Rainfall is also easily observed by young children. They can create a simple scale that goes from not raining to raining lightly (drizzling) to raining hard (downpour).

A More Accurate Rain Gauge ► *Activity 34*

DEVELOPMENTAL LEVEL
1–3

GROUP SIZE
Small

KEY EXPERIENCES

• *Measuring, testing, and analyzing: assessing the properties and composition of materials*

• *Designing, building, fabricating, and modifying structures or materials*

• *Reporting and interpreting data and results*

Children can also make a simple rain gauge, giving more exact measurements in inches, and compare their readings with published weather data. The dimensions of the rain gauge are important. The collecting bottle should be 2" (5 cm) in diameter and at least 10" (25 cm) high. The funnel should be 4" (10 cm) in diameter. Students should paste or tape a scale on the outside of the bottle to get direct readings (see Illustration 35). Have them place the gauge in a safe but open place outside the school. To prevent the gauge from being blown over, put it in a weighted tin or sink it in the ground. Set up a schedule for students to observe and record the amount of rainfall. Have them compare their results to news reports or listings in the newspaper.

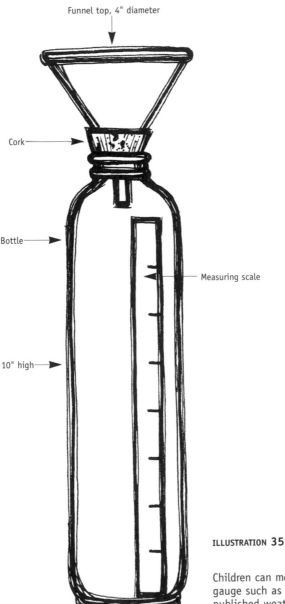

Funnel top, 4" diameter

Cork

Bottle

Measuring scale

10" high

2" wide

ILLUSTRATION 35

Making a Rain Gauge

Children can measure the amount of rainfall with a simple gauge such as this and compare their findings with published weather data.

Wind Direction ▶ *Activity 35*

DEVELOPMENTAL LEVEL
K–2

GROUP SIZE
Large

KEY EXPERIENCES

- *Observing, predicting, and controlling change: understanding causality*

- *Designing, building, fabricating, and modifying structures or materials*

- *Reporting and interpreting data and results*

Students can easily make a windsock to indicate the direction of the wind. The open end of a nylon sock should be sewn around a hoop and the edges of the hoop attached to a pole with two pieces of nylon twine or thin string (see Illustration 36). Students can mark the directions (N, S, E, W) on the ground or at the top of the pole and sink the pole into the ground far enough to be steady. As they see the sock move with the wind, discuss which direction the wind is coming *from* and how it make the windsock blow in the opposite direction.

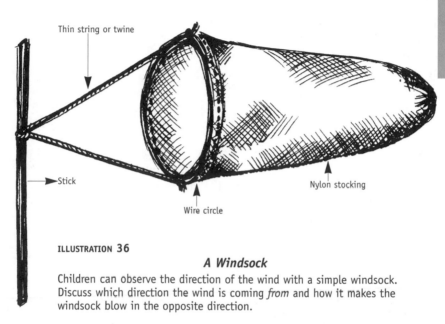

Thin string or twine

Stick

Wire circle

Nylon stocking

ILLUSTRATION 36

A Windsock

Children can observe the direction of the wind with a simple windsock. Discuss which direction the wind is coming *from* and how it makes the windsock blow in the opposite direction.

Wind Speed ► *Activity 36*

DEVELOPMENTAL LEVEL
3–5

GROUP SIZE
Small

KEY EXPERIENCES

- *Measuring, testing, and analyzing: assessing the properties and composition of materials*

- *Observing, predicting, and controlling change: understanding causality*

- *Designing, building, fabricating, and modifying structures or materials*

- *Reporting and interpreting data and results*

___ A NOTE FOR TEACHERS ___

The Beaufort Scale

The Beaufort scale is made up of a series of numbers that correspond to descriptions of the observable effects of wind. The numbers can be used to indicate an estimated wind speed. The scale was worked out in approximately 1805 by the British Rear naval office Sir Francis Beaufort. He defined the numbers in terms of the wind's effect on sailing vessels. It was intended for use by sailors and referred to the sails of a fully rigged frigate. Since that time, the Beaufort numbers have been adopted all over the world, and their values have been standardized. Using the scale produces a fair estimate of the wind speed even when no instruments are available. The observer uses the movement of the clouds, trees, smoke, and birds to provide a guide to wind speed. The Beaufort scale is also a useful guide when calibrating homemade anemometers.

Wind speed can be estimated using a simple, swinging gate anemometer that has been calibrated against the Beaufort scale. To make this anemometer, children will need a knitting needle, a thin material to act as a flap, a wooden base, and an L-shaped upright (two walls) on one side of which they have attached a scale on a curve (see Illustration 37).

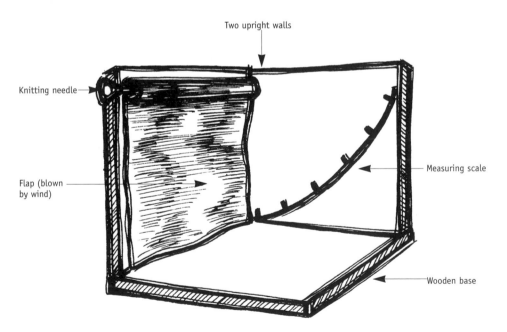

ILLUSTRATION 37

A Swinging Gate Anemometer

At first, children can measure the speed of the wind using their own measuring scale; later, teachers can introduce the units of the Beaufort scale.

At first, children can mark this scale in intervals of their own devising to record wind speeds. Later, the units of the Beaufort scale can be introduced, as shown in the chart below. Students also may be interested to learn of the origins of the scale and Admiral Beaufort's life as a sailor.

A SIMPLIFIED BEAUFORT SCALE

Force	Description	Wind Speed in MPH
0. Calm	Smoke rises vertically	Less than 1
1. Light air	Smoke drift can be seen	1–3
2. Light breeze	Wind felt on face; leaves rustle	4–7
3. Gentle breeze	Leaves in constant motion, flags flutter in wind	8–12
4. Moderate breeze	Raises dust, loose paper blows, small branches move	13–18
5. Fresh breeze	Small trees begin to sway	19–24
6. Strong breeze	Large branches sway, whistling of the wind in overhead wires	25–31
7. Moderate gale	Whole trees sway; hard to walk against the wind	32–38
8. Fresh gale	Twigs break from trees	39–49
9. Gale	Branches fall from trees, buildings are damaged	50–60
10. Strong gale	Considerable damage	61–70
11. Storm	Widespread damage	71–75
12. Hurricane	Devastation	Above 75

Changes in Visibility ▶ *Activity 37*

DEVELOPMENTAL LEVEL
K–2

GROUP SIZE
Large

KEY EXPERIENCES

• *Looking with a purpose: observing and collecting data*

• *Observing, predicting, and controlling change: understanding causality*

• *Reporting and interpreting data and results*

Changes in visibility can be interesting to observe both over a day and over a week. Choose local landmarks and have students invent a scale to record poor, moderate, and good visibility. For example, students can pick favorite sights and indicate how clearly they can see them from a given location. More ambitious visibility scales can be made using a local map to pinpoint distant landmarks at such distances as $\frac{1}{4}$, $\frac{1}{2}$, 2, 4, and 6 miles. It is especially useful to make such observations from a high point, such as the top floor of a tall school building or a nearby building or hill.

Seasonal Changes ▶ *Activity 38*

DEVELOPMENTAL LEVEL
K–2

GROUP SIZE
Large

KEY EXPERIENCES

- *Looking with a purpose: observing and collecting data*

- *Observing, predicting, and controlling change: understanding causality*

- *Reporting and interpreting data and results*

Seasonal changes are obvious once children become aware of them. Biological examples—from collections or observations or records— can help to bring seasonal changes into focus. Begin with human signs of the season and then bring in animal and plant changes. The following examples of seasonal changes can be explored in various ways.

• *Seasonal changes in human patterns.* Have students observe and describe changes in their clothing, the routes they take to and from school (for example, snow routes in winter or dirt roads to be avoided in muddy spring weather), the kinds of foods available at different times of year, our dependence on natural versus artificial light, and the use of indoor and outdoor leisure time.

• *Seasonal changes in animals.* Students can observe and keep records of changes in the appearance of animals (for example, the thickness of fur or the color of feathers), in their habits (such as birds building nests in spring or storing food for the winter), and in the presence or absence of certain animals in a given area (for example, birds migrating to, or returning from, the south). Small animals—spiders, snails, worms—are excellent to study. Have students pick a specific geographical area and record the changes in animal life that they see over several months.

• *Seasonal changes in plants.* Students can keep records of trees, bushes, and flowering plants in a designated area. They can record such things as the color and presence of foliage and changes in the appearance of bark and twigs. For a focused study, students might observe one plant through a seed cycle or a fruiting cycle.

Part Seven

Change in the Garden

Making a garden and observing its changes is a universal activity appropriate for children of all developmental levels. Gardens provide the basis for an ongoing project around the year, and gardening activities can be used to cover all the science key experiences. Remember, however, that even a small school garden will be an ongoing responsibility, one which requires regular attention. Don't harvest all of the crops, however. Let some go to seed so that children can see different stages in the cycle of change. Change is epitomized in the garden. Use it as a resource in science.

***Planting a
School Garden***
► Activity 39 — p. 77

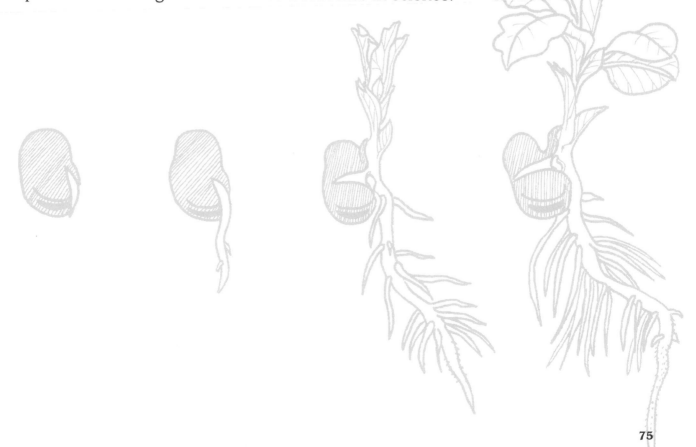

School Gardens

School gardens should be planned and used, not as places where gardening techniques are taught, but as a place for exploration, observation, and experimentation. The aim will not be to produce good crops or be limited to beautifying the school site, but rather to provide the focus for active learning about plants, birds, insects, weather, and soil. Sometimes the unhealthy plant with a population of caterpillars or aphids on it will be of more educational interest than a perfect specimen. To maximize these educational opportunities, the garden should have many spaces where children plant seeds of their own choice and carry out a wide variety of observations and activities.

School gardens are best kept small and easily accessible, preferably with a hard surfaced path to one side of the plot and mulched paths (for example, covered with straw) throughout. Ideally, the garden or its surrounding area should have trees at different stages of growth from young to mature. Shrubs planted singly or in groups provide an opportunity to study color, shape, and bird and insect life. If the school site has an area for a wild garden, so much the better. Here the natural vegetation can take over, together with the birds, mammals, and insects whose homes are there. Keep working paths through such an area so that observation is easy without destroying the wild life it is intended to encourage.

Keep in mind the cyclical nature of opportunities presented by the school garden and its surroundings:

• *Fall.* Autumn fruits and leaves; small animals of the soil, such as spiders; bird populations and their changes

• *Winter.* Appearance of twigs and bark; presence and behavior of birds

• *Spring.* Changes in trees, especially deciduous varieties; small plants and their development; soft-bodied animals and overwintering insects

• *Summer.* Summer birds; weeds, wild flowers, and waste places; butterflies, moths, and flies; trees and shrubs

Teachers can adapt the preceding list to the climate and location provided by their own school setting.

Planting a School Garden ▶ *Activity 39*

DEVELOPMENTAL LEVEL
K–6

GROUP SIZE
Small and Large

KEY EXPERIENCES

- *Looking with a purpose: observing and collecting data*

- *Classifying and ordering materials according to their attributes and properties*

- *Measuring, testing, and analyzing: assessing the properties and composition of materials*

- *Observing, predicting, and controlling change: understanding causality*

- *Designing, building, fabricating, and modifying structures or materials*

- *Reporting and interpreting data and results*

When planting a school garden, there are ten considerations to keep in mind:

1. Be sure you really want to do it. Planting and maintaining a garden is a year-round responsibility.

2. Plan a garden that children can manage. Keep it small.

3. Plan a garden that will allow children to experience the cycles of the year.

4. Select a plot with good soil. Poor soil—with little germination and growth—is very discouraging and provides little opportunity for observation. If good soil is not available, see about having some good soil brought in for a small plot. If this is not feasible, find nearby natural areas and study the cycles of wild vegetation in the area. Supplement this study by planting some seeds indoors and examining the growing cycle.

5. Use only new and good seeds. Old seeds, even if they appear to be packed well, may not germinate.

6. Follow the directions for planting on the seed packet with care and attention.

7. Plant according to the contours of the land—not up and down a slope, but around its curves.

8. Keep the cultivation going. Remove weeds as soon as they are identified. If the students are interested in studying weeds, either keep a designated area of the garden for this purpose or identify additional wild areas near the garden.

9. Take care when watering the garden. Too much water can be as bad as too little.

10. Keep a record of procedures and results. Have students keep garden diaries or post a chart on the wall so that all students can record what they did and what they observed on a daily basis.

The chart below lists some suitable plants that are easy to grow and that provide opportunities for year-round study.

PLANTING A SCHOOL GARDEN

Flower or Vegetable	Planting Depth	Space Between Plants	Space Between Rows
Bean	2"	8"	18"
Beet	1"	4"	12"
Carrot	1/2"	3"	12"
Lettuce	1/2"	3"	12"
Radish	1/2"	2"	12"
Marigold	1/2"	12"	12"
Zinnia	1/2"	12"	12"

Part Eight

Diversity in Change

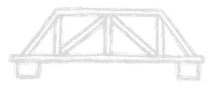

S tudying the changes that take place all around us everyday in our world can be a fascinating and worthwhile investigation for children. From changes in humans to changes in color to physical and chemical changes, the diversity of topics to explore is endless.

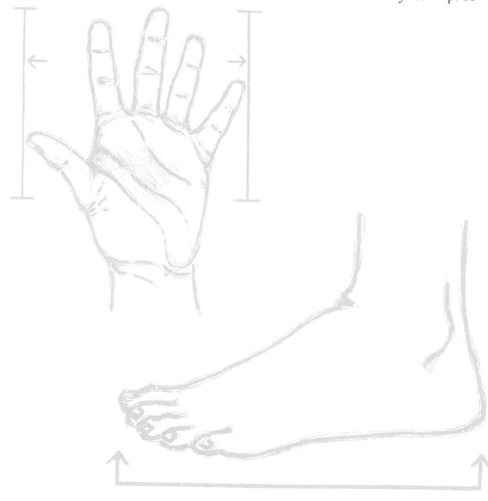

Human Change ▶ *Activity 40*

DEVELOPMENTAL LEVEL
K–2

GROUP SIZE
Large

KEY EXPERIENCES

• *Looking with a purpose: observing and collecting data*

• *Reporting and interpreting data and results*

Human change is an excellent topic for investigation because children can begin by studying themselves. Children can keep records of naturally occurring changes over the course of the school year—height, weight, circumference of head, length of feet, and size of hands. They can also investigate the kinds of change (improvement) brought about by practice—writing with the nondominant hand, learning a new skill such as roller skating or riding a bicycle, or tossing bags into a bucket at different distances. Discuss with students how they can tell when change has taken place. What do they observe on the outside? Do they feel different about themselves and their abilities on the inside? Is change always an improvement? What are the conditions that affect change?

Color Change ▶ *Activity 41*

DEVELOPMENTAL LEVEL
1–3

GROUP SIZE
Large

KEY EXPERIENCES

• *Looking with a purpose: observing and collecting data*

• *Observing, predicting, and controlling change: understanding causality*

• *Reporting and interpreting data and results*

There are many opportunities for children to investigate color change. Students can examine color variations in the same kind of flower, color changes in lichens and moss under different weather conditions, color changes in clouds and rainbows. Students can also investigate how colors affect one another. For example, they can observe how the colors of cars change under different color street lights. They can record their results on a chart such as the one below.

How the Colors of Cars Change Under Different Color Street Lights

Color of Car in Daylight	Color of Car Seen Under Different Street Lights		
	Yellow Street Light	Blue Street Light	White Street Light
Black			
White			
Red			
Blue			
Yellow			
Green			
Other Colors:			

Students can also study color changes in the home. For example, they can look at the fading of fabrics, paints, and wallpapers. Discuss with them what causes fading and whether certain materials and colors fade more than others. Students can devise methods for measuring and recording the amount of fading. Students can also experiment with changing colors by dyeing fabric (use cold-water dyes for this purpose) or using vegetable dyes to change the colors of foods. They can investigate how color can be used to highlight or hide other colors. For example, have them place colored squares against different color backgrounds and observe the effects from different distances. What background colors make an object of a given color stand out? What background colors help to camouflage or hide an object of a given color? How can we use our knowledge of how colors change one another, for example, in designing clothes or tools or safety devices?

Physical Change ▶ *Activity 42*

DEVELOPMENTAL LEVEL
K–2

GROUP SIZE
Large

KEY EXPERIENCES

- *Looking with a purpose: observing and collecting data*

- *Measuring, testing, and analyzing: assessing the properties and composition of materials*

- *Observing, predicting, and controlling change: understanding causality*

- *Reporting and interpreting data and results*

Students can investigate *physical* change in all three areas of the science curriculum—life and environment, structure and form, and energy and change. Use these investigations to explore the ideas of stability and change, equilibrium, movement, and constancy and variability. Here are some activities for studying change:

• *Wind.* Students can look at changes brought about by the wind, such as trees leaning with the prevailing wind, dust clouds kicked up by the wind during dry spells, leaves blown off trees, or litter blown around the street.

• *Clothing.* Children can study clothing to observe changes due to shifting fashions, seasonal weather changes, or differences in the dress of people of different ages.

• *Toys and simple machines.* Children can observe the interaction of mechanical parts in toys and simple machines. Have them discuss how moving or changing one part causes changes in the position or action of another part.

• *Speed.* Children can investigate changes in speed from many different angles. How does nature bring about changes in speed? For example, how quickly do fruits and vegetables ripen? How fast do different animals reach maturity? How do people change the speed of objects and processes, for example, by mechanical means of generating energy or by devoting more time to an activity?

• *Sound.* Students can do many things that bring about changes in sound. How does the structure and shape of musical instruments allow us to produce different sounds? Have students explore such sound-changing activities as tapping, banging, blowing, plucking, and bowing.

• *Shape.* Students can investigate how changes in shape bring about changes in performance. For example, they can make paper gliders and kites to study how changing the shape influences flight patterns and speed. They can look at similarities and differences in the shapes of common objects that serve the same purpose, for example, different shapes of roofs, bridges, houses, and cars.

Chemical Change ▶ *Activity 43*

DEVELOPMENTAL LEVEL
2–4

GROUP SIZE

Small

KEY EXPERIENCES

• *Measuring, testing, and analyzing: assessing the properties and composition of materials*

• *Observing, predicting, and controlling change: understanding causality*

• *Designing, building, fabricating, and modifying structures or materials*

• *Reporting and interpreting data and results*

Everyday activities provide opportunities for students to study chemical change. One of the themes to examine is whether these changes are permanent or temporary. For example, students can explore changes brought about by heat and by water. Cooking, an activity that students enjoy, is another good way to examine chemical change.

• *Heat.* Have students observe and describe the changes that happen when things are heated on a warm radiator or in the hot sun. For example, what are the conditions under which ice cubes melt? What happens if a pinch of salt is put on one of the ice cubes? Have students listen and look. What happens to water when it is exposed to heat? What happens when milk is boiled, then cooled? Does it look the same or taste the same? Is the change permanent? What change happens to an egg when it is boiled? Is the change permanent? How is toast different from bread? Is the change brought about by toasting permanent?

• *Water.* Students can examine chemical changes by drying objects and then reversing the process. For example, have them soak fruits and vegetables (prunes, apricots, peas, beans). What happens after two hours of soaking? After overnight soaking? Compare the soaked items with the originals. How do they differ in size, texture, or taste? Does the water they are soaked in change as well? Washing can also provide an occasion for observation and comparisons. Have students try washing dirty hands in cold water with no soap, in cold water with soap, and in warm water with soap. What are the results? Which condition creates the most bubbles? Which condition removes the most dirt? Have the students wash dirty, greasy dishes. Again, which condition (cold versus warm water, with and without detergent) works the best? Students can try dissolving different substances in water. Discuss whether these substances have disappeared forever or changed their form. Have them put saucers of solutions in the sun or on a radiator to see what happens after the water evaporates. Students can make a table of solubility for kitchen food and chemicals, such as the one below. Have them invent ways of testing solubility that are fair, for example, by systematically varying the amount of water or the number of stirs for each substance.

Solubility of Kitchen Foods and Chemicals

Soluble: Dissolves Quickly	Not Very Soluble: Dissolves Slowly	Insoluble: Does Not Dissolve
Sugar	Baking soda	Scouring powder
Salt		Pepper
Epsom salts		Flour
Laundry detergent		Oats

• *Cooking.* Have students prepare a simple recipe, such as this one for short-bread.

Observing Changes by Cooking an Easy Recipe: Shortbread

Ingredients:

8 oz (225 gms) flour	2 oz (55 gms) sugar
1 oz (115 gms) butter	¼ tsp. salt

Procedure:
Soften butter. Sieve flour, sugar, and salt into mixing bowl, rub ingredients with tips of fingers until well mixed. Knead mixture until it forms a ball. Press evenly into a greased tin. Prick with a fork. Cook at 350° F for 30 minutes. [**Note:** An adult should take the tin out of the oven.]

Look carefully at the individual ingredients before cooking. Compare the finished product with its components. What changes can be observed in physical appearance—size, shape, texture, color? How does the taste of individual ingredients before cooking compare to the taste of the combined finished product after cooking? What brings about these changes? Discuss processes in the kitchen—dissolving, stirring, soaking, chopping, heating, and cooling—that bring about change.

Part Nine

Electrical Energy

E lectrical energy is an important and ever-present element in daily life. Children are generally aware of its role in powering the sophisticated equipment with which they are surrounded in their schools and homes. However, the complexity of the equipment prevents children from appreciating the nature of electrical energy and how it can be controlled, manipulated, and incorporated in their own work. The activities in this section allow children to create simple circuits and control devices as they experiment with batteries, bulbs, and wires.

Electricity

The term *electricity* comes from the Greek word "elector," which means "sun." Virtually everything is electrical in nature. All matter consists of atoms, and each atom has one or more electrons and one or more protons. These tiny particles have equal but opposite charges of electricity—protons are positively charged and electrons are negatively charged. Protons are heavier than electrons and are bound tightly to the centers of the atoms. Only electrons can move freely. Ordinarily an atom is neutral—neither positive nor negative in charge—because it has an equal number of electrons and protons. But if an atom gains electrons, it becomes negatively charged; if it loses electrons, it becomes positively charged. Charged atoms always attract uncharged atoms.

There are two kinds of electricity—*static electricity* and *current electricity.* In static electricity, electrons are not moving from one atom to another. In current electricity, electrons are moving from one atom to another. It is static electricity that makes hair crackle when it is combed on a day when the air is dry. Static electricity can be produced by rubbing a comb with a piece of wool. The atoms in the wool lose some of their electrons and the atoms in the comb gain them. If you put the comb near some small pieces of paper they will be attracted to it. The pieces of paper have no charge (they are neutral) and are therefore attracted to the positively charged comb.

Current electricity has many more uses than static electricity. Current electricity works for us by powering all kinds of devices and machines. In order to conduct electricity, a substance must have electrons that are free to move from atom to atom. Metals have such free electrons and so they make good conductors of electricity. In some materials, such as rubber and glass, the electrons are so tightly bound to the atoms that few can move. These materials are poor conductors or nonconductors. Instead, they can serve as insulators when we want to prevent the flow or loss of electrical energy.

The flow of an electric current depends on three factors: the pressure which causes the electrons to flow; the rate at which they flow; and the resistance of the wire to the flow. It is this flow that produces the power of electricity. The units used to measure these three factors are named after famous scientists: *volts* measure pressure; *amperes* measure the amount or rate of current flow; and *ohms* measure resistance. The total power is measured in *watts.*

Electricity from batteries is safe and usually low in power, whereas the electricity from the main power supply is high powered and can be dangerous. Using safe low-powered sources of electrical energy, teachers can introduce children to many simple activities. For example, students can cause changes in electrical effects, control the flow of electric current, and design simple circuits to meet the needs created by their own improvisation and experimentation.

A Simple Circuit ▶ *Activity 44*

DEVELOPMENTAL LEVEL
K–2

GROUP SIZE
Small

KEY EXPERIENCES

• *Measuring, testing, and analyzing: assessing the properties and composition of materials*

• *Observing, predicting, and controlling change: understanding causality*

• *Designing, building, fabricating, and modifying structures or materials*

• *Reporting and interpreting data and results*

To begin this activity provide students with lengths of wire (single-strand bell wire with the insulation remaining on the ends), bulbs in bulb holders, and a battery (see Illustration 38).

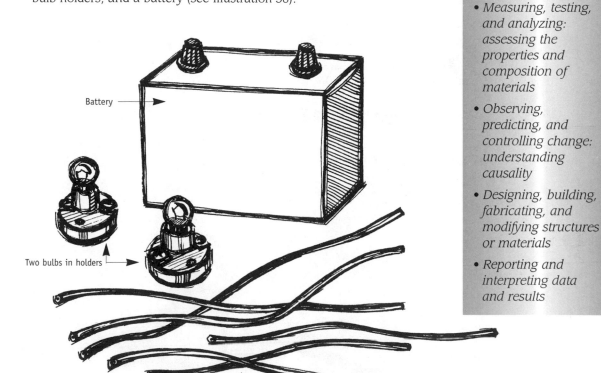

Battery

Two bulbs in holders

Single-strand bell wire with the insulation remaining on the ends

ILLUSTRATION 38

Materials for a Simple Circuit
Children can make a simple circuit with lengths of wire, bulbs in bulb holders, and a battery. As they experiment with these materials, they may discover that the insulation around the wires makes electrical contact difficult.

Ask the children if they can make the lights come on. Let them try to link the bulb holders to the battery. As they experiment, point out that the screw contacts have a purpose. Let them discover that the insulation around the wire makes it difficult to secure the ends of the wire to the battery and to make electrical contact. If necessary, show students how to remove the insulation from the wire (see Illustration 39).

Bare wire

Insulation

End bent for easy contact

ILLUSTRATION 39

Removing Insulation From Wires
After removing the insulation from the ends of the wires, students should bend them into a hook shape.

After the insulation has been removed from the ends of the wire to provide good contacts, have students bend the wire into a hook shape to go around the contact screws. This will enable them to attach the wires to the battery; after some trial and error, the light will come on. Let students secure the connections by tightening the screws attached to both the battery and the bulb holder (see Illustration 40). Have children draw the plan of the circuit they made. If possible, see if children in another class can follow these plans to create their own circuits.

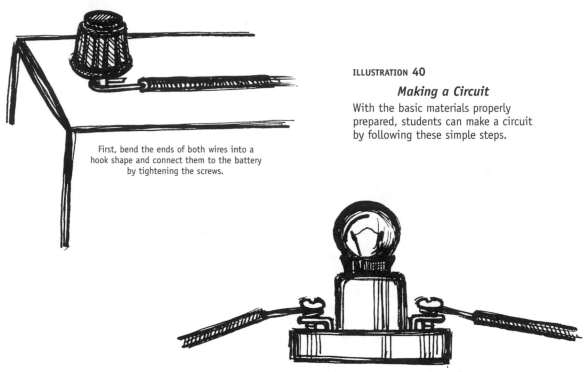

First, bend the ends of both wires into a hook shape and connect them to the battery by tightening the screws.

ILLUSTRATION 40

Making a Circuit
With the basic materials properly prepared, students can make a circuit by following these simple steps.

Attach the other ends of the wires to either side of the bulb holder, fastening them in place by tightening the screws.

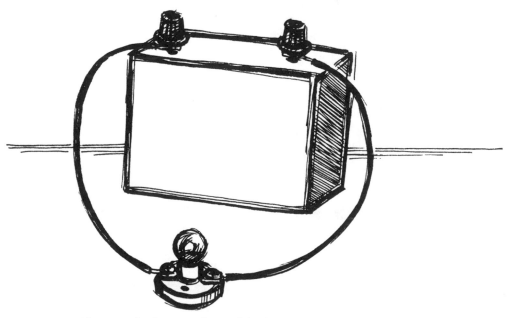

After some trail and error to make sure all the wires are connected, the light will come on.

A Simple Switch ▶ *Activity 45*

DEVELOPMENTAL LEVEL
1–3

GROUP SIZE
Small

KEY EXPERIENCES

- *Measuring, testing, and analyzing: assessing the properties and composition of materials*

- *Observing, predicting, and controlling change: understanding causality*

- *Designing, building, fabricating, and modifying structures or materials*

- *Reporting and interpreting data and results*

Students can use blocks of wood, thumbtacks, and long paper clips to invent a simple switch. One end of the paper clip—the switch—should be put under one thumbtack pressed into a block of wood. Have them experiment to connect the bare end of one wire under the thumbtack with the paper clip switch. Have them experiment to connect the other end of a bare wire to a second thumbtack pressed into the block of wood. When the paper clip switch is "on," the free end should touch the second thumbtack. They can discover that the other ends of the wires should be attached to one of the screws of the battery and to the bulb. The metal thumbtacks act as the electrical contacts to make the switch work (see Illustration 41).

Have the children draw a plan of the circuits they have made and see if children in another class can use the plan to create their own circuits.

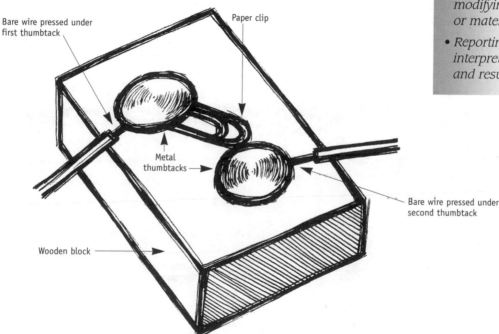

Bare wire pressed under first thumbtack

Paper clip

Metal thumbtacks

Bare wire pressed under second thumbtack

Wooden block

ILLUSTRATION 41

Making a Simple Switch
Using blocks of wood, thumbtacks, and long paper clips, students can invent a simple switch.

Simple Bulb Holders and Switches ▶ *Activity 46*

DEVELOPMENTAL LEVEL
2–4

GROUP SIZE
Small

KEY EXPERIENCES

- *Measuring, testing, and analyzing: assessing the properties and composition of materials*

- *Observing, predicting, and controlling change: understanding causality*

- *Designing, building, fabricating, and modifying structures or materials*

- *Reporting and interpreting data and results*

Children can invent and construct many different types of bulb holders and switches (see Illustration 42 below and on pg. 91). To make one type of a simple bulb holder, for example, students can twist together two wires and hold them in place with cellophane tape. The insulation at the ends of the wires should be removed. Enough insulation should be removed at the end of one of the wires so that it can be twisted into a coil wide enough to contain the end of the bulb.

Students can use a clothespin to make another simple bulb holder. Have them insert a bulb with a wire contact into the end of the open clothespin. When the grip is released and the clothespin tightens, it holds the wire in contact. Another wire is taped to the base of the bulb. Finally, a cork can be used to make a switching mechanism similar to the one in Illustration 41. Have them attach the wire along two sides of the cork, using staples. Strip the ends of the wires, bending one of them into a hook over the other wire. Pressing down on the hook or releasing it will act as a switch to turn the light on or off as it touches the second contact wire.

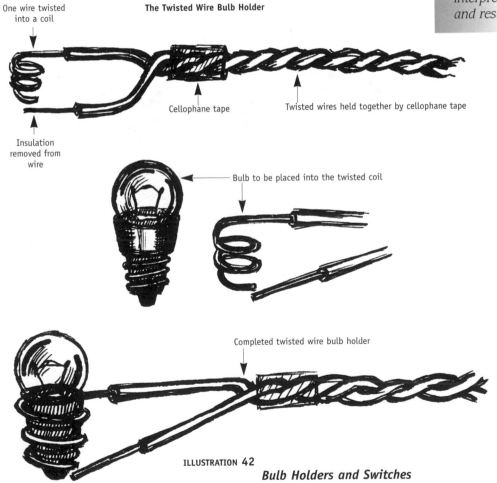

The Twisted Wire Bulb Holder

One wire twisted into a coil

Cellophane tape

Twisted wires held together by cellophane tape

Insulation removed from wire

Bulb to be placed into the twisted coil

Completed twisted wire bulb holder

ILLUSTRATION 42
Bulb Holders and Switches

Children can use a variety of materials to invent and construct many different types of bulb holders and switches.

The Clothespin Bulb Holder

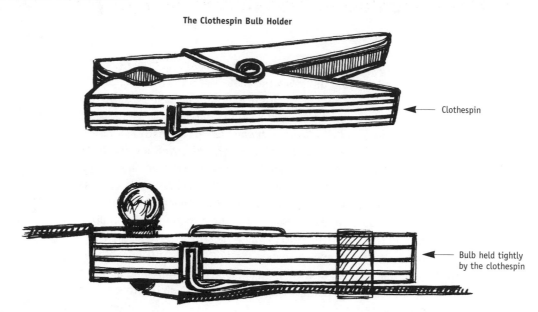

Clothespin

Bulb held tightly
by the clothespin

The Cork Switch

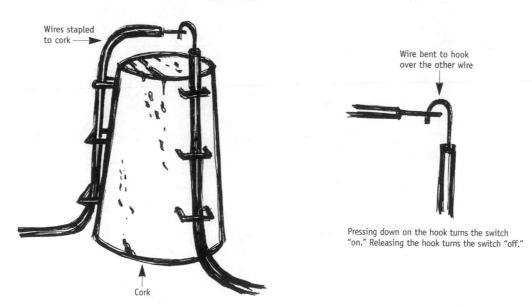

Wires stapled
to cork

Cork

Wire bent to hook
over the other wire

Pressing down on the hook turns the switch
"on." Releasing the hook turns the switch "off."

Using Simple Circuits—the Box House
▶ *Activity 47*

Making simple circuits will help children understand how their homes are lit. Using the following materials and construction processes, students can make a box house lit by electricity. The bulb holders and paper clip switches created in the previous activities can be used in the box house. Each floor of the house can be made out of a shoebox with a rectangular opening cut out that is covered with clear plastic for the windows. Have students cut a hole in the lid of each box for the bulb holder and bulb. The bulb should be pushed down on the inside of the lid (the side facing toward the open box), and the bulb holder should be taped in place on the top. Have them attach a bulb to each floor of the house and then attach the wires to a battery. The multiple sets of wires running between the battery and the house will begin to give students an idea of the complexity of wiring and lighting an entire home. If the students wish, they can add switches to the circuits (see Illustration 43).

DEVELOPMENTAL LEVEL
2–4

GROUP SIZE
Small

KEY EXPERIENCES

• *Measuring, testing, and analyzing: assessing the properties and composition of materials*

• *Observing, predicting, and controlling change: understanding causality*

• *Designing, building, fabricating, and modifying structures or materials*

• *Reporting and interpreting data and results*

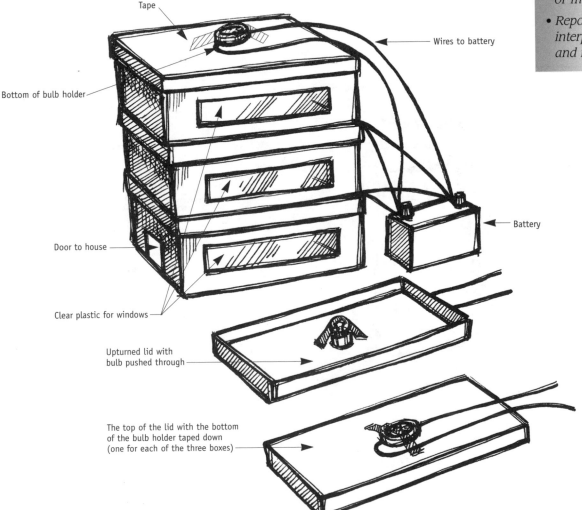

Tape

Wires to battery

Bottom of bulb holder

Battery

Door to house

Clear plastic for windows

Upturned lid with bulb pushed through

The top of the lid with the bottom of the bulb holder taped down (one for each of the three boxes)

ILLUSTRATION 43

Using a Simple Circuit to Light a Three-Story Box House
Making simple circuits can help young children understand how their homes are lit by electricity.

The Egg Carton Traffic Light ▶ *Activity 48*

DEVELOPMENTAL LEVEL
1–3

GROUP SIZE
Small

KEY EXPERIENCES

• *Measuring, testing, and analyzing: assessing the properties and composition of materials*

• *Observing, predicting, and controlling change: understanding causality*

• *Designing, building, fabricating, and modifying structures or materials*

• *Reporting and interpreting data and results*

Children can also see how simple circuits work by making an egg carton traffic light. Two bulbs are set in holders, and the glass part is pushed through the bulbous end of the egg carton. The holders are taped in place and covered with red and green tissue paper, also held in place with tape. Attach the bare ends of the wires to the bulb's base and side contacts and the other ends of the wires to the battery. Using the paper clip switch created earlier, students can operate the traffic light. Have them invent various "stop and go" games using the red and green lights (see Illustration 44).

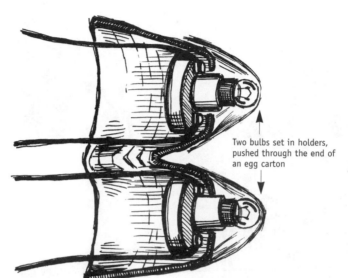

Two bulbs set in holders, pushed through the end of an egg carton

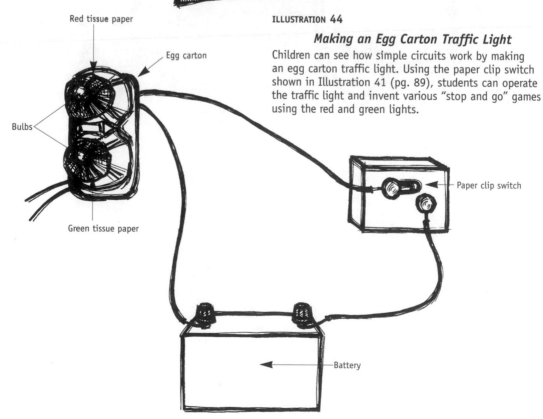

Red tissue paper

Egg carton

Bulbs

Green tissue paper

Paper clip switch

Battery

ILLUSTRATION 44

Making an Egg Carton Traffic Light

Children can see how simple circuits work by making an egg carton traffic light. Using the paper clip switch shown in Illustration 41 (pg. 89), students can operate the traffic light and invent various "stop and go" games using the red and green lights.

The Pocket Light ▶ *Activity 49*

DEVELOPMENTAL LEVEL
1–3

GROUP SIZE
Large

KEY EXPERIENCES

• *Measuring, testing, and analyzing: assessing the properties and composition of materials*

• *Observing, predicting, and controlling change: understanding causality*

• *Designing, building, fabricating, and modifying structures or materials*

• *Reporting and interpreting data and results*

The pocket light is another example of a simple circuit that students can make. Using a single-cell battery, students insert the bulb into the coiled wire on top. Tape around the sides holds the wire firmly in place against the top contact of the battery. To make the light come on, students press the other end of the wire to the battery base (see Illustration 45).

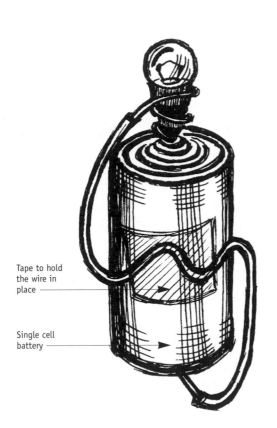

Tape to hold
the wire in
place

Single cell
battery

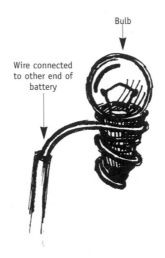

Bulb

Wire connected
to other end of
battery

ILLUSTRATION 45

The Pocket Light

To make a pocket light, students insert a bulb into the coiled wire on top of a single-cell battery. After taping around the sides to hold the wire firmly in place, students can press the other end of the wire to the battery base to make the light come on.

The Airport Beacon Light With Signal Control
► *Activity 50*

Making an airport beacon light shows another use of a simple circuit. Students will need an empty plastic bottle, wire, a battery, and the bulb holders and paper clip switch they made before. The bulb holder is taped to the top of the plastic bottle with wires connected to the contacts. Two holes are cut near the top of the bottle for the wires to go into the bulb holder, and one hole is cut near the bottom for the wires to exit to the switch and battery. One wire is attached to the paper clip switch and the other to the battery. A third wire connects the battery to the second thumbtack on the wooden block of the switch. When the paper clip is touched to the second thumbtack, making the connection, the bulb will be lit (see Illustration 46).

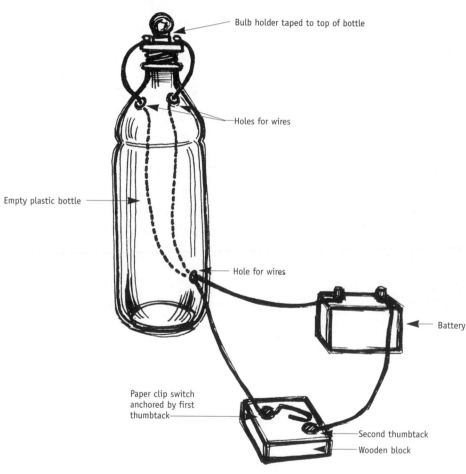

Bulb holder taped to top of bottle

Holes for wires

Empty plastic bottle

Hole for wires

Battery

Paper clip switch anchored by first thumbtack

Second thumbtack

Wooden block

Paper clip opened and bent to make a switch key, anchored under first thumbtack

Second thumbtack for paper clip to touch in "on" position

ILLUSTRATION 46

Making an Airport Beacon Light
Making an airport beacon with a signal control shows another use of a simple circuit.

DEVELOPMENTAL LEVEL
1–3

GROUP SIZE
Small

KEY EXPERIENCES

• *Measuring, testing, and analyzing: assessing the properties and composition of materials*

• *Observing, predicting, and controlling change: understanding causality*

• *Designing, building, fabricating, and modifying structures or materials*

• *Reporting and interpreting data and results*

Part Ten

Energy From Magnets and Magnetism

*M*agnetism is a force that acts between objects. All magnets are surrounded by magnetic fields, including the Earth, which is itself a giant magnet at its core. Simple elements of magnetic force can be explored and investigated by even young children.

Making Compasses From Magnets
► Activity 51 — p. 99

Magnetism and Magnets

Scientists theorize that there are huge electric currents deep within the earth and that these currents in some way produce magnetism. The first known magnets were naturally occurring ones—hard black pieces of rock called lodestones. The ancient Greeks knew that lodestone would attract iron. During the Middle Ages, it was known that a suspended lodestone would swing to point to the North. In the seventeenth century, William Gilbert discovered that the Earth's magnetism explained the action of the compass. But it was not until Hans Christian Oersted discovered in 1819 that an electric current could move a compass needle that real progress in using this force came about. Michael Faraday took this work forward ten years later when he discovered that moving a magnet in a coil produced an electric current. This relationship between electricity and magnetism paved the way for the development of the modern electrical machines we accept as part of daily life.

Some milestones in the discovery of the properties and uses of magnetism and electricity:

1749   Benjamin Franklin discovered that lightning was similar to electric sparks.

1780   Luigi Galvani discovered current electricity.

1800   Alessandro Volta converted chemical energy into electrical energy.

1819   Hans Christian Oersted discovered the action of an electric current on a magnet.

1829   Joseph Henry made the first electromagnet.

1831   Michael Faraday discovered the principle of the dynamo.

These discoveries, spanning nearly a century, have opened the way for modern studies into magnetism. Although scientists are still discovering what this force is, the principles of magnetism are used in the manufacture of many products today.

Making Compasses From Magnets ▶ *Activity 51*

DEVELOPMENTAL LEVEL
1–3

GROUP SIZE
Small

KEY EXPERIENCES

• *Measuring, testing, and analyzing: assessing the properties and composition of materials*

• *Designing, building, fabricating, and modifying structures or materials*

• *Reporting and interpreting data and results*

Making compasses from magnets is something children can do successfully with little equipment. The first step is to magnetize the metal that will serve as the compass needle. Have students try different metals and compare the results. Suitable items to try include steel knitting needles or darning needles with blunt ends, pieces of steel strip, and nails made of iron versus other metals. The important thing to remember in magnetizing the metal from another stronger magnet is that the stroking of the metal to be magnetized must be in one direction. Have the students magnetize different metals and see how effective they are by picking up pins or iron tacks (see Illustration 47).

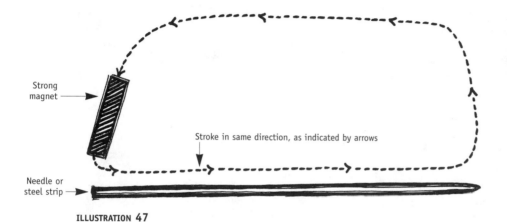

Strong magnet

Stroke in same direction, as indicated by arrows

Needle or steel strip

ILLUSTRATION 47

Using a Magnet to Make a Compass

The first step in making a compass is to magnetize the metal that will serve as the compass needle. To magnetize the metal, stroke the needle with the magnet. Remember: the strokes must all be in the same direction.

To make a compass, have students magnetize a darning needle very well. Again, test the magnetism by picking up small iron objects. Cut a piece of polystyrene large enough to place the magnetized needle on and fix the needle in the center with a small piece of cellophane tape. Next, have students get a plastic dish or bowl with a little water in it, just enough to float the piece of polystyrene (see Illustration 48). As the polystyrene floats on the water, have them watch which way the needle points. Let them put the bowl in several different places in the room. In what direction does the needle point? Is it still the same direction? Students can compare the compass they have made with a pocket compass.

Mark an "N" on the dish (needle always points north)

N

Magnetized needle

Piece of polystyrene

Plastic dish filled with water

ILLUSTRATION 48

Testing the Compass

To test the compass, tape the magnetized needle onto a piece of polystyrene. As the polystyrene floats on the water, students can observe that the needle always points north, no matter how they turn or move the dish.

Next, students can use this float setup to observe the actions of other types of magnets. For example, how does a strong flat magnet (not a horseshoe magnet) behave? What about a cylindrical magnet?

Students can make another type of compass from a circular box lid, two magnetized strips, a needle, a snap fastener, and a lump of clay (see Illustration 49). Have them test the compasses in several different places and establish routes around the classroom and the school using compass directions. Let them investigate other activities using their sense of directions. For example, students can record where the sun rises and how it moves throughout the day or the directions in which automobile or air traffic noises originate and fade.

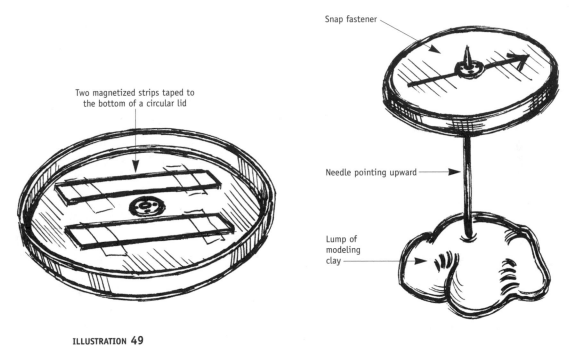

Snap fastener

Two magnetized strips taped to the bottom of a circular lid

Needle pointing upward

Lump of modeling clay

ILLUSTRATION **49**

Observing Other Types of Magnets

Students can make and observe other types of magnets, such as this cylindrical magnet made from a circular box lid, two magnetized strips, a needle, a snap fastener, and a lump of clay.

Part Eleven

Energy and Change Case Studies: Some Classroom Experiences

The following cases studies describe what happens when ideas on paper or in the teacher's mind are actually used with children. Teachers begin a science project with specific learning experiences in mind. While students may indeed generate these experiences, their own interests will also lead to the development of other activities and insights. The classroom experiences presented in this section provide real-life examples of how planned activities may evolve into unanticipated explorations in science. In all cases, the children are actively engaged, and the teacher is flexible enough to respond to the students' leads. The resulting learning is rich, varied, and exciting.

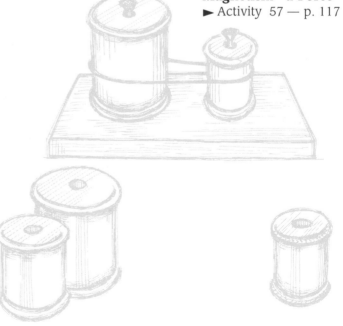

Work and Force—Work Is a Push or a Pull and Needs Energy ▶ *Activity 52*

DEVELOPMENTAL LEVEL
K–2

GROUP SIZE
Large

KEY EXPERIENCES

- *Measuring, testing, and analyzing: assessing the properties and composition of materials*

- *Designing, building, fabricating, and modifying structures or materials*

- *Reporting and interpreting data and results*

General Experiences the Teacher Had in Mind

- To enable children to experience that work requires effort (energy)

- To help children to see that machines can make work easier and help us use less of our own energy

Other Experiences the Teacher Hoped to Encourage

- To experience force and effort (push and pull) firsthand

- To see how children can use their force to move a very heavy load

- To bring about situations in which students could think how to make a task easier

- To introduce the concept of measuring force, starting with crude measures such as how many children it takes to push or pull a load

- To refine the idea of measuring the force using a spring balance connected to a pulling rope

Follow-up Activities the Teacher Hoped to Stimulate

- To get children to compare pushing versus pulling as a way to move a load a given distance

- To introduce simple mechanical devices (such as rollers created from broom handles) to make it easier to move a load

- To calibrate a spring balance (7–56 pounds or 5–25 kilograms) and discuss how it could be used to measure the amount of force needed with different energy-saving devices

Activities That Actually Resulted

- The teacher provided a wooden box loaded with house bricks. The box had a smooth, but not polished, bottom. Children took turns trying to push it alone but no one could. Children tried working with a partner to push the box; some pairs could and other pairs could not. Children tried in groups of three to push the box, and all groups were able to do it.

- The result was discussed. Students agreed that "child power" (the number of children needed to move the box) was a measure of force. It was also thought that a set distance should be fixed over which the load should be moved. Three feet was chosen and marked on the floor.

- The teacher attached a rope firmly to the box and the children tried pulling it this time. Again, they worked singly, in two's, and in three's, using the same combinations of children to make a fair comparison.

• Children put the results in a chart and discussed the amount of energy needed for pushing versus pulling.

• The teacher put two broomsticks under the loaded box, and children repeated the pushing and pulling singly, in two's, and in three's. The results were recorded and discussed.

• The whole activity captivated the children's imagination to the extent they wanted to continue their testing the next day. The teacher brought in a spring balance and inserted it in the rope. The above procedures were repeated using the measurements on the balance and recording and discussing them. Discussion brought out an appreciation of force and how sliding is more difficult than rolling. Children noted that shiny, slippery floor surfaces might give very different results.

Work and Machines—Wheels and Simple Machines ► *Activity 53*

General Experiences the Teacher Had in Mind

- To examine wheels as simple machines

- To provide firsthand experience of the use of wheels in real and child-invented devices

Other Experiences the Teacher Hoped to Encourage

- To appreciate that rolling friction is less than sliding friction and that wheels are a means of bringing about rolling friction

- To see that some wheels turn other wheels in machines and to examine what happens when small wheels turn large wheels and vice versa

- To discover that the pulley is another use for wheels

Follow-up Activities the Teacher Hoped to Stimulate

- To pull a load by sliding it on the ground versus putting the load on a skateboard and then pulling it; to estimate this comparison by hand and then use a spring balance inserted in the pulling cord to make comparative measurements of the force needed; to describe and tabulate the results

- To make a simple trolley—with and without wheels—for transporting a load using everyday items such as thread spools, nails, and a small wooden box (see Illustration 50)

DEVELOPMENTAL LEVEL
2–4

GROUP SIZE
Small

KEY EXPERIENCES

- *Measuring, testing, and analyzing: assessing the properties and composition of materials*

- *Observing, predicting, and controlling change: understanding causality*

- *Designing, building, fabricating, and modifying structures or materials*

- *Reporting and interpreting data and results*

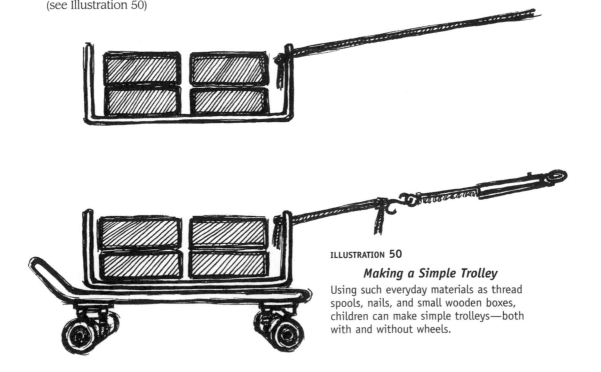

ILLUSTRATION 50

Making a Simple Trolley

Using such everyday materials as thread spools, nails, and small wooden boxes, children can make simple trolleys—both with and without wheels.

• To discover how wheels can turn each other; to observe the direction of the turning

• To investigate how wheels are used in toys, for example, in clockwork toys

• To observe how the pulley on a flagpole makes it easy to put up the flag

Activities That Actually Resulted

• One group of children set up a large-scale experiment to investigate friction and the use of wheels to compare sliding motion and rolling motion. The experiment involved a box loaded with four house bricks pulled by a rope. Various children in the group tested the pull needed to move it. The loaded box was put onto a skateboard, the rope was attached, and the pull needed was tested again. The teacher showed students how to insert a spring scale into the pulling rope. Students repeated the experiment and measured the results. They made charts to illustrate and display their work.

• A second group of children tested smaller scale loads using cigar-box carts and toy trucks. A sloping plank was used to test uphill pulls. The teacher showed students how to use a spring scale to measure the pulls. Students drew pictures to record the results and discussed their activities (see Illustration 51).

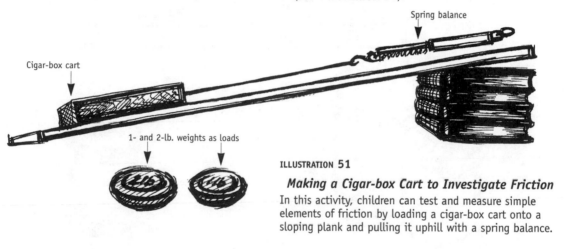

ILLUSTRATION **51**

Making a Cigar-box Cart to Investigate Friction
In this activity, children can test and measure simple elements of friction by loading a cigar-box cart onto a sloping plank and pulling it uphill with a spring balance.

• A third group of children investigated how wheels can turn other wheels. They used various sizes of spools and same-size bottlecaps, nails for spindles, and pieces of wood for the bases. The children invented wheels turning each other by touching (friction drives) as well as being connected by elastic bands (see Illustration 52 on pg. 106). They had large wheels driving small wheels and the reverse. It was exciting for children to realize that they had created the transmission of motion. The teacher posed the following questions to the group studying wheels:

1. What happens to the direction of motion when one wheel drives another?

2. When a large wheel drives a small wheel, what happens to the speed at which the small wheel turns?

3. When a small wheel drives a large wheel, what happens to the speed at which the large wheel turns?

4. What happens when a band drive is fixed not straight over each reel, but crossed over in the middle?

• The next day there was a lively discussion of the three sets of experiments. The teacher had intended to steer the work back to such problems as "How does the pulley do a useful job?" The class, however, was more intent on further investigation of wheels and energy. The class put together a large selection of simple mechanisms with wheels—toy cars, old clocks, eggbeaters, and model trains. Each group used its new knowledge of wheels to look critically at these specimens and then report their observations about how things worked to the whole class. The standard of reporting and communicating was very high; students offered intelligent guesses when they were unable to observe mechanisms directly. The teacher's role was a mixture of enabler, encourager, leader, and supplier. She judged well when to mix her experiences with the children's. The result was very good science education.

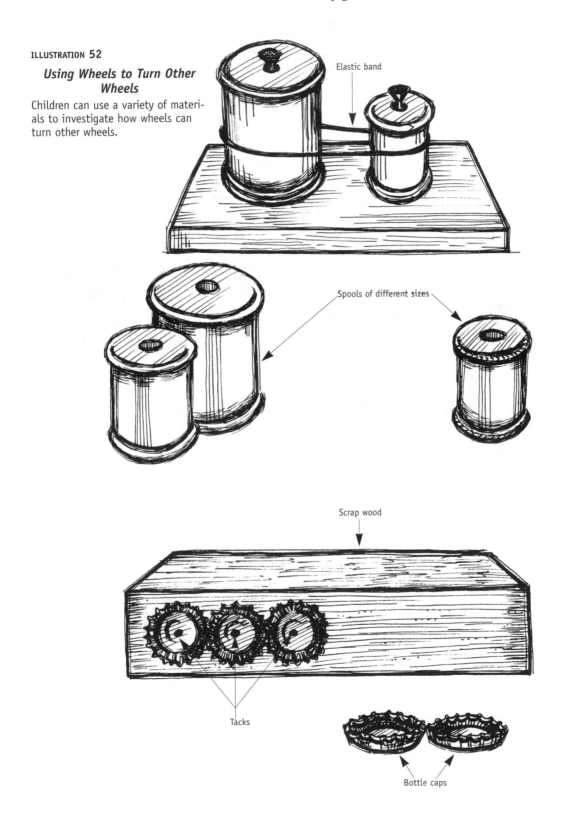

ILLUSTRATION 52

Using Wheels to Turn Other Wheels

Children can use a variety of materials to investigate how wheels can turn other wheels.

Elastic band

Spools of different sizes

Scrap wood

Tacks

Bottle caps

Work and Machines—The Great Tractor Trials
► *Activity 54*

DEVELOPMENTAL LEVEL
1–3

GROUP SIZE
Small

KEY EXPERIENCES

• *Measuring, testing, and analyzing: assessing the properties and composition of materials*

• *Observing, predicting, and controlling change: understanding causality*

• *Designing, building, fabricating, and modifying structures or materials*

• *Reporting and interpreting data and results*

General Experiences the Teacher Had in Mind

• To introduce the idea of measuring the performance of toy tractors, beginning with arbitrary standards and refining these standards as the work progressed

Other Experiences the Teacher Hoped to Encourage

• To give more precision to the measurement of "farthest" and "fastest"

• To invent standard loads for "power trials"

• To find ways to communicate the results of hill trials

Follow-up Activities the Teacher Hoped to Stimulate

• To have students consider how they could make the comparisons fair; to devise a fair test, such as the best 3 out of 5 trials

• To have students consider how to measure attributes in addition to speed

• To develop different methods of displaying the results

Activities That Actually Resulted

• The group began with a straight course for racing the tractors down the hallway. The race course did not have a length limit. Students lined up the tractors at the starting point and the race began. Problems soon arose in interpreting the results. The fastest tractors did not go as far as the slower tractors. What sort of result was this? Students invented new rules for the race. They created a short course for speed trials and a long course for endurance trials. The new sets of results were noted and discussed.

• Out of these discussions the idea of testing "strength" grew. It was decided to try load pulling. A test cart to carry a load was found in the toy box. The teacher helped make a universal coupling out of metal paper clips. Students decided that small wooden cubes fit well into the cart and could be used as a measurable load. Trials were held and the results were recorded in terms of the number of cubes carried.

Change—Time, Timing, and Timers ▶ *Activity 55*

DEVELOPMENTAL LEVEL
3–5

GROUP SIZE
Small

KEY EXPERIENCES

• *Measuring, testing, and analyzing: assessing the properties and composition of materials*

• *Observing, predicting, and controlling change: understanding causality*

• *Designing, building, fabricating, and modifying structures or materials*

• *Reporting and interpreting data and results*

General Experiences the Teacher Had in Mind

• To appreciate two aspects of the concept of time—the sequence of events and the duration of events

Other Experiences the Teacher Hoped to Encourage

• To order common events in sequence; to make visual representations as picture clocks, beginning with broad sequences (for example, getting up, getting dressed, eating breakfast) and progressing to events within the sequence (for example, the order in which clothes are put on; the sequence of actions to tie a shoelace)

• To time how long activities take (for example, walking down a corridor, hopping from one end of the room to the other); to compare the duration of various activities (for example, walking and running times over a set distance in the playground)

Follow-up Activities the Teacher Hoped to Stimulate

• To become familiar with different types of clocks to measure time

• To create different timing devices and use them to record the results of timing tests

• To measure personal times for reaction times, pulse, and respiration rates

• To see the relationship between time and the sun using sundials and shadow clocks

• To become aware of and record cycles of time during the day, the school year, and the seasons

• To experience time as tempo, that is, musical time

Activities That Actually Resulted

• The teacher made available a variety of timing devices. He provided a seconds timer, a stop clock, a stopwatch, a metronome set to beat half-seconds, an alarm clock, and an egg timer.

• One group of children made a picture clock of the sequences of their day. They used a circular format to show it as a repeating cycle of activities during the week (see Illustration 53 on pg. 109). The circle had a day and night division indicated by a light versus dark background. No attempt was made to assign a time duration to the activities. However, there were more day-time activities around the circle, which gave children a sense of the longer duration of waking hours.

ILLUSTRATION 53

Creating a Picture Clock

Children can use a circle such as this one to visually display the repeating cycle of activities that make up their day. Although activities are not assigned a particular time duration, the picture clock gives children a sense of the longer duration of daytime events.

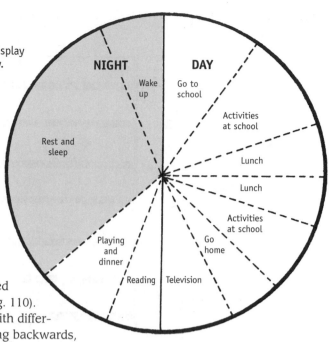

• Another group of children made a picture chart of the sequence of actions needed to open the main school door first thing in the morning (see Illustration 54).

• Timing the duration of events with a stopwatch occupied several groups. For example, one group set up a course around the playground and then timed the duration of walking versus running around it. They recorded these results on a chart (see Illustration 55 on pg. 110). Other children tried going around the course with different forms of motion—hopping, skipping, walking backwards, three-legged races, and so on. They discussed which method took the least time and which took the most time.

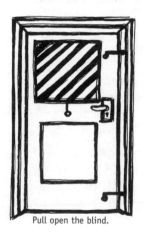

Pull open the blind.

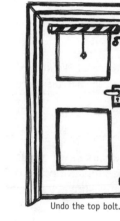

Undo the top bolt.

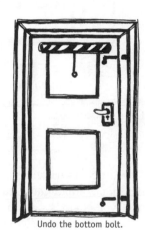

Undo the bottom bolt.

ILLUSTRATION 54

A Sequence for Unlocking a Door in the Morning

Children can create pictures that show the sequence of events needed to open the main school door in the morning. Discuss with them that these actions are reversed when locking the door again at night.

Turn the key.

Turn the handle.

Open the door.

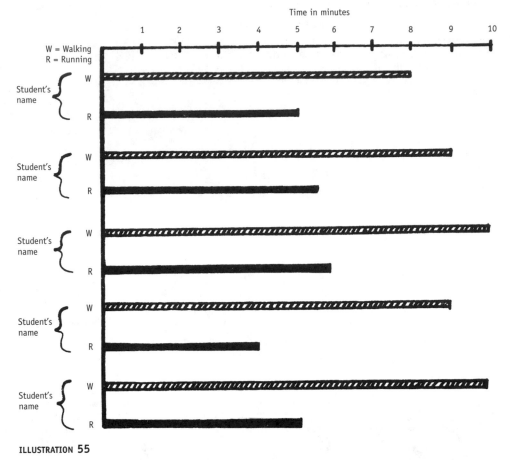

ILLUSTRATION 55

Timing the Duration of Events: Walking Versus Running

Students can set up a course around the playground and then time how long it takes them to walk and then run around it.

• Students made a variety of water clocks—a regular water clock, a Chinese water clock, and a giant water clock (see Illustration 56 on pg. 111). They discussed which type of clock was appropriate to measure activities of short duration and which type activities of long duration.

• Students made and tested sundials of various designs. Some students set up a shadow stick in the playground and took measurements of the length of the sun's shadow every half-hour. The next day, they presented these results as a histogram (see Illustration 57 on pg 112).

• Students used the human pulse to measure time, counting the number of beats it took to complete various activities. They timed their respiration after walking a course and after running the course once, twice, and three times around.

• Students made a survey of timing aids that could be used when a timer was not available. This list included the windshield wipers on a car; flashing lights on aircraft; sirens on emergency vehicles; changing colors on a traffic light; and blinking lights on neon signs. The list was displayed on a large wall chart with the heading: Can you supply the time for these flashing lights?

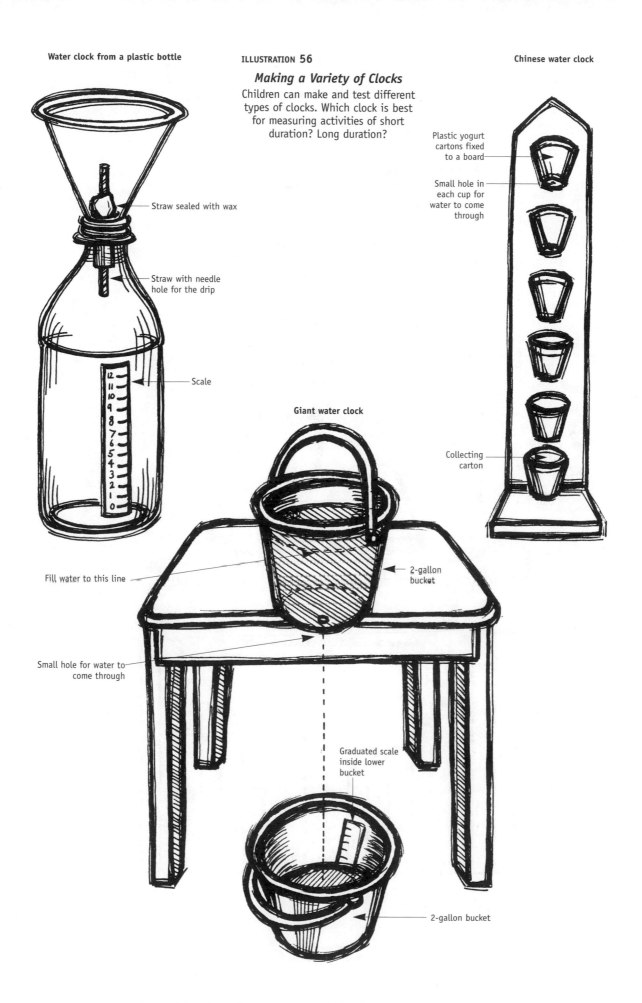

Water clock from a plastic bottle

ILLUSTRATION 56

Making a Variety of Clocks

Children can make and test different types of clocks. Which clock is best for measuring activities of short duration? Long duration?

Chinese water clock

Straw sealed with wax

Straw with needle hole for the drip

Scale

Plastic yogurt cartons fixed to a board

Small hole in each cup for water to come through

Collecting carton

Giant water clock

Fill water to this line

Small hole for water to come through

2-gallon bucket

Graduated scale inside lower bucket

2-gallon bucket

ENERGY AND CHANGE CASE STUDIES: SOME CLASSROOM EXPERIENCES

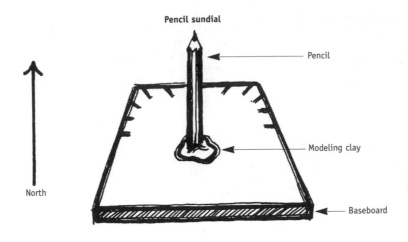

Pencil sundial

Pencil

Modeling clay

North

Baseboard

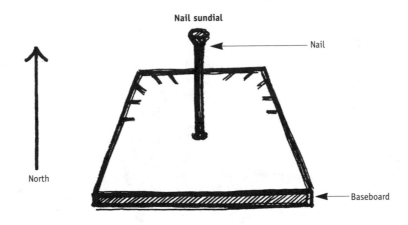

Nail sundial

Nail

North

Baseboard

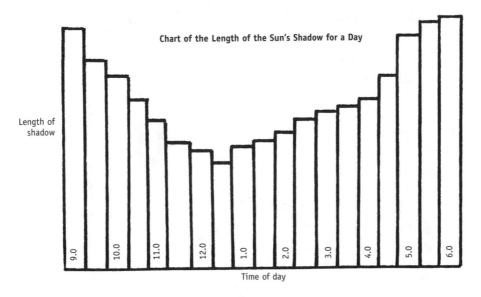

Chart of the Length of the Sun's Shadow for a Day

Length of shadow

9.0 | 10.0 | 11.0 | 12.0 | 1.0 | 2.0 | 3.0 | 4.0 | 5.0 | 6.0

Time of day

ILLUSTRATION 57

Sundials

Students can make and test sundials of various designs. After setting up a pencil or nail sundial on the playground, children can make a chart to show their findings.

Energy Conversion and Use—Current Electricity in Circuits ▶ *Activity 56*

DEVELOPMENTAL LEVEL
4–6

GROUP SIZE
Large

KEY EXPERIENCES

- *Measuring, testing, and analyzing: assessing the properties and composition of materials*

- *Observing, predicting, and controlling change: understanding causality*

- *Designing, building, fabricating, and modifying structures or materials*

- *Reporting and interpreting data and results*

General Experiences the Teacher Had in Mind

- To construct three lamp circuits using simple equipment

- To gain some knowledge of how to control current electricity

- To become familiar with the design of circuits, switches, and insulation

Other Experiences the Teacher Hoped to Encourage

- To stimulate and encourage improvisation with simple materials in constructing the apparatus needed for experiments

- To use the simple electrical circuit to appreciate the route current electricity takes in a simple circuit and the role played by the insulation of wires in a circuit

- To study conductors and nonconductors of electricity

- To invent switching devices for a simple circuit

- To experiment with different methods of connecting three lights in a circuit, that is, series and parallel connections

Follow-up Activities the Teacher Hoped to Stimulate

- To discover the basic pattern of a simple circuit by manipulating connections between battery and bulb; to isolate the essential facts that there are two connections to the bulb and two on the battery

- To compare the use of bare wire versus insulated wire in a simple circuit; to pose the following questions about the use of insulated wire: (1) What happens when the insulation is removed? (2) What else could act as an insulator? (3) Can a simple way of testing conductors and insulators be devised?

- To devise ways of making bulb holders so that circuits can be built up more easily

- To devise connectors and connections using wires, paper clips, thumbtacks, and cardboard or wooden bases

- To invent a switch and experiment with switches in the circuit

- To use more than one light in the circuit and explore different circuit patterns (that is, serial and parallel circuits)

Activities That Actually Resulted

The teacher made the following materials available: batteries, bulbs, clothespins, corks, 1" nails, bulb holders, thumbtacks, bare wire, insulated wire, pieces of cardboard and wood for bases (about 2" × 3" or 5 cm × 8 cm), cellophane tape, paper clips, aluminum foil, empty matchboxes, and a box of scrap materials for testing for conductivity. The teacher made the following tools available: wire strippers, small hammers, scissors, rulers, and small screwdrivers.

• Children experimented with the bare wire, battery, and bulb to find the connection that completes the circuit and lights the bulb. They isolated the important elements in the contacts—the two for the bulb and the two for the battery. Children made simple drawings of the circuits so that other students in the class could make them if they wished.

• Students made a set of three bulb holders and experimented with different ways of connecting them in parallel and series circuits. They made drawings of the circuits. They discussed which type of circuit gave the best light and which gave the worst (see Illustration 58 below and on pg. 115).

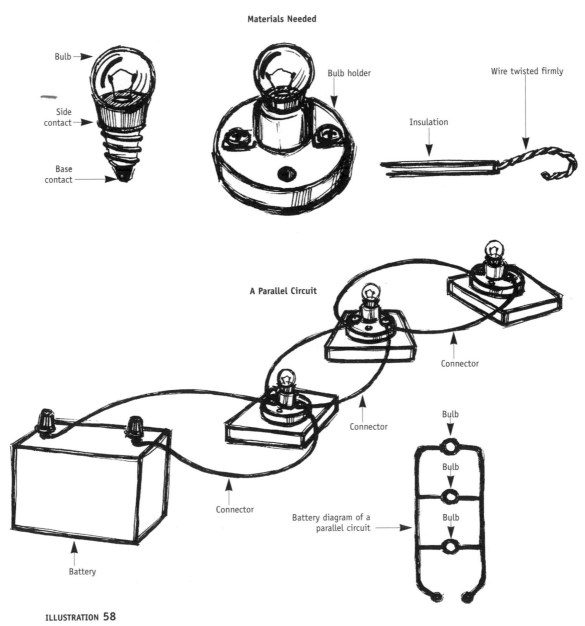

Materials Needed

Bulb

Side contact

Base contact

Bulb holder

Wire twisted firmly

Insulation

A Parallel Circuit

Connector

Connector

Connector

Bulb

Bulb

Bulb

Battery diagram of a parallel circuit

Battery

ILLUSTRATION **58**

Experimenting With Circuits

Students can explore many properties of electrical energy by experimenting with different ways of connecting bulb holders in parallel and series circuits.

A Series Circuit

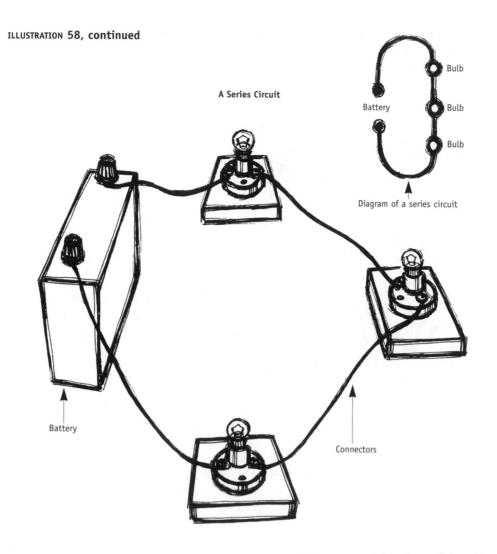

Battery

Bulb

Bulb

Bulb

Diagram of a series circuit

Battery

Connectors

• Children experimented with the bare wire and the insulated wire. They discussed problems that arose with the insulated wire. They investigated what happens in the circuit when the insulation is removed from the contact ends of the wire. Students used the available tools and materials to turn the bare wire into insulated wire.

• Students made a simple switch to turn the light on and off using paper clips, thumbtacks, and a wooden block (see Illustration 59).

ILLUSTRATION **59**

A Paper Clip Connector

Students can make a simple switch to turn lights on and off using such everyday items as paper clips, thumbtacks, and wooden blocks.

ENERGY AND CHANGE CASE STUDIES: SOME CLASSROOM EXPERIENCES

• Students invented bulb holders using corks and nails or clothespins. They used the bulb holders they invented to make a simple circuit. They made the circuit more secure by fixing the battery to a block of wood with cellophane tape. Students tried using metal paper clips as connectors (see Illustration 60).

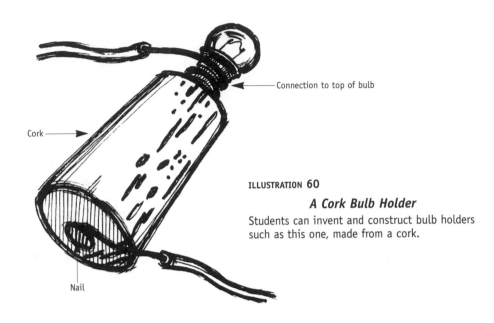

Connection to top of bulb

Cork

Nail

ILLUSTRATION 60

A Cork Bulb Holder

Students can invent and construct bulb holders such as this one, made from a cork.

• Students made a conductivity testing board with light circuits consisting of bulb holders and connector wires of different lengths. To test the conductors, they bridged the gap between the thumbtacks with the metal paper clip switch. They also tried different materials in the space between the thumbtacks to see how well these materials conducted electricity (see Illustration 61).

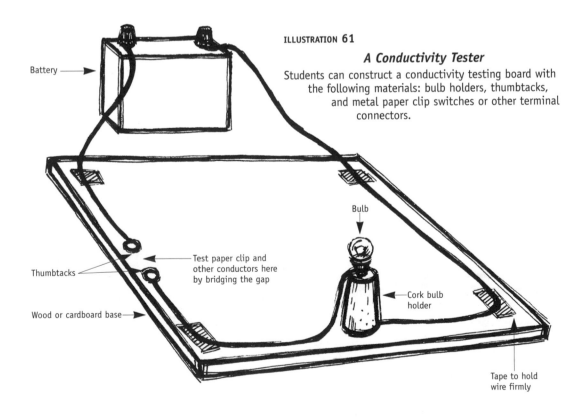

ILLUSTRATION 61

A Conductivity Tester

Students can construct a conductivity testing board with the following materials: bulb holders, thumbtacks, and metal paper clip switches or other terminal connectors.

Battery

Bulb

Test paper clip and other conductors here by bridging the gap

Thumbtacks

Cork bulb holder

Wood or cardboard base

Tape to hold wire firmly

Magnetism—A Force ▶ *Activity 57*

DEVELOPMENTAL LEVEL
1–3

GROUP SIZE
Small

KEY EXPERIENCES

• *Measuring, testing, and analyzing: assessing the properties and composition of materials*

• *Observing, predicting, and controlling change: understanding causality*

• *Designing, building, fabricating, and modifying structures or materials*

• *Reporting and interpreting data and results*

General Experiences the Teacher Had in Mind

- To experience and appreciate magnetic force
- To use the energy of magnetic force in simple experiments

Other Experiences the Teacher Hoped to Encourage

- To discover which materials are attracted by a magnet and which are not

- To discover conditions (such as coverings) that affect magnetic attraction

- To find out that magnets have polarity; to find out the effects of polarity when magnets react with one another

- To invent simple uses for magnets, for example, fishing games (catching ferrous objects) and steering games (steering a paper clip "car" with a magnet, steering a model boat)

Follow-up Activities the Teacher Hoped to Stimulate

- To play with pairs of magnets to discover the phenomenon of polarity and its effects

- To discover how magnets behave with one another; to experience magnetic attraction and repulsion

Activities That Actually Resulted

- Children played with pairs of magnets, holding them together, reversing them one at a time, and then gently moving them apart. The magnets were placed on the smooth tabletop, one was gradually brought near the other, and the effect was noted. Then one magnet was reversed and the effect noted. The ends of the magnets were both marked "x" when they pushed apart. The teacher initiated a discussion of these observations by asking, "Is there a pattern to these results?"

- The children tried picking up things with their magnets. They experimented with different types of materials and with different sizes of objects. The teacher produced boxes containing small ferrous objects; ferrous objects coated with brass, plastic, paint, and paper; and other materials including wood, plastic, paper, aluminum foil, cloth, feathers, and corks. The children used the magnets to sort this material in two piles—"picked up" and "not picked up."

- The teacher initiated a discussion of the results. The fact that magnets attracted ferrous objects soon emerged. The fact that apparently nonferrous objects were also attracted was explored further. Working in small groups, the children experimented with the materials and concluded that ferrous objects coated with other substances could also be attracted to magnets.

• Students invented a steering game using magnets. The teacher provided the following materials: flat pieces of polystyrene cut in boat shapes, thin nails 1¼" long, toothpicks cut in half, tape, and large bowls of water. Students used these materials along with a set of simple instructions to construct a boat—they taped the nail to the polystyrene and put a paper sail on the toothpick as the mast. They used their magnets to steer their boats, investigating different positions for the magnet to see which produced the best effects (see Illustration 62).

ILLUSTRATION **62**

Using Magnets to Steer a Boat

Children can explore simple properties of magnetic energy in a variety of interesting ways. In this activity, they use a magnet to steer a boat, investigating which position produces the best effects.

Teaching Aids

This Teaching Aids appendix covers a range of topics that teachers will find useful as they prepare science education activities for children to carry out. Five areas are addressed:

• *Communication techniques for the classroom.* This section is divided into two parts. The first part provides the teacher with pointers on how to help children order and interpret information. The second part discusses how teachers can help children communicate and display the information that results from their science activities.

• *Materials and equipment.* This section emphasizes how teachers and children can use what is readily available to conduct science activities. Although the specific materials needed for each activity are described in the body of the text, this section encourages the use of commonplace materials to make discoveries about the world around us. A list of simple tools and equipment that teachers will find handy is provided.

• *Measurement in science.* There are two parts to the measurement section. The first part discusses measurement techniques and simple timing and weighing devices that are useful to have in the classroom. The second part describes the use of, and conversion to, metric measures—the standard measurement system of science.

• *Testing and analysis.* This section illustrates the process of testing and analyzing the properties of various animate and inanimate materials in the classroom.

• *Safety and science.* Safety must be an essential consideration in all aspects of education, perhaps most especially so in the area of science. Children will be working with unfamiliar materials, or with commonplace materials in unfamiliar ways. This section describes basic procedures and safety precautions that teachers and students should be aware of as they carry out the science activities.

Part 1

Communication Techniques for the Classroom

Ordering and Interpreting Information

Making Surveys

Surveys are a form of collecting—collecting information. The usefulness of the activity will depend upon the interpretation and communication of the results by the collectors. There are many interesting subjects to survey and many ways to present the results. Following are some examples. The techniques described for communicating results in the early examples can also be applied to the suggestions in the later examples.

Collecting Personal Statistics From Members of the Class or Group

Some suggested collections include: ages, heights, weights, hand spans, shoe sizes, addresses for distance from the school, modes of transportation, hobbies, books students have read, pets, favorite colors, sweets, foods, names, and initials. The educational value of this work is enhanced greatly by the manner of presenting the results. These facts will be quantitative in one or more of their aspects; they are records of counting or some kind of measuring. They may be collected in no special order and may appear haphazard. Therefore, to be effectively communicated, that is, to see the significance of such results, they must be arranged and presented in ways that will show some pattern. This can be a regular sequence from the smallest to largest, or a trend, as in the case of the popularity of certain hobbies. Some useful ways of presenting information are given below. Teachers will note that there is a clear overlap with mathematics in this area of science activities.

Presenting Sets

When children have collected the information they desire and want to communicate it to others, they may provide suitable pictures and group these as pictures or symbols within an enclosed boundary. When two sets have some connection, they can be compared and the correspondences indicated by arrows, e.g., size of shoes and size of feet. Comparisons can be made more obvious if the sets are represented on graph paper. Place one element in each square, in columns, with the elements side by side. With this arrangement, matches can be seen at a glance.

Establishing an Order

There are many ways of ordering information—numerically, alphabetically, by visual arrangement. Once children understand the concept of *counting order,* they have a technique for sequencing that enables them to order by matching things to numbers. For example, the record of the numbers of birthdays occurring each month may be listed in this way. Another method of ordering is alphabetical. This can be used for surveys of names, comparing first names and second names in separate listings. Sometimes information is best presented as a rectangular array chart. This could be used for a survey of favorite colors or candies (see table below).

	George	Mary	Sue	John	William	Jane	Jack	Warren	Kay
Black									
Yellow	√	√		√	√	√	√		√
Blue		√				√		√	
Green	√		√			√			√
Red			√	√	√		√	√	√
White	√		√					√	
Brown		√		√	√		√		

When larger numbers are involved, a continuation of several individual surveys can be made to give numerical summaries.

Tabulating Results

Charts. When a large number of measurements have been taken, such as the heights of each child in the class, students can construct a chart to represent the results. The first job will be to put the results in order from smallest to tallest. Such a long list is not easy to study, but the results can be interpreted using markers; for example, by observing how many heights are above the chosen marker and how many are below. Results can also be grouped for clarity. For example, students can make a chart showing the ranges of heights and the numbers in that range (see Illustration A1). This could also be displayed on graph paper as a chart.

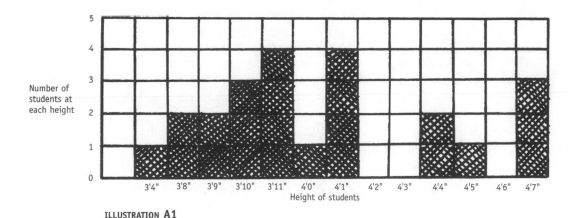

ILLUSTRATION A1

Chart Showing Height Range

Students take measurements and arrange the results in order to make a graph of heights in the classroom.

Pictograms. It is sometimes easier to represent information in pictorial form with symbolic figures such as ships, cars, stick figures, cats, dogs, and so on (see Illustration A2 on pg. 122). For younger children learning to count, letting one symbol represent each instance helps them to learn one-to-one correspondence. For older children, one picture or symbol can represent a number of facts; for example, each

ILLUSTRATION **A2**

Chart of Children's Pets
On this chart, one picture represents three pets.

book pictured can represent five books read. Using one to symbolize many is also a more sophisticated and efficient way of representing data, since it avoids the problem of having the space in the chart too crowded with symbols.

Pie graphs. A portioned or divided circle is a valuable way of showing how different pieces of information make up the whole picture. This type of representation is commonly called a pie chart (see Illustration A3). Children quickly learn how to mark out a clock face and divide the circle accordingly. There are many occasions when a class will find a pie chart the most telling way of exhibiting information, for example, the different means of transportation that children use to get to school. The limitation of the pie chart is that it does not lend itself to the comparison of two similar situations.

ILLUSTRATION **A3**

Pie Graph of How Children Get to School

A pie graph is a valuable way of showing how different pieces of information make up the whole picture.

Examples

The following examples will provide data that can be treated using the above ordering and interpretation techniques. Examples like these will be found throughout the books in this series.

Wildlife in an area. This information can be collected on a variety of topics. For example, data can be recorded on the total number of birds or the number of birds of different species seen at given times. Statistics could also be collected on the number of mammals seen, the number of insects observed in an area, or the number of spider webs. The statistics can relate to an area generally, such as the grounds outside the school, or to specific locations, such as a bird-feeding table.

Plant life in an area. Students can count and record various aspects of plant life. For example, surveys might include the total number of trees, the number of each of a certain type of small plant, weeds in a lawn, or seeds on seed heads of particular plants. More ambitious projects will involve inventing units of measurement for such tasks as estimating the number of leaves or apples on a tree, berries on a bush, or even flowers on a lawn or in a flower bed. Surveys of this type involve mathematical skills such as estimating and using one to represent many.

Materials used in buildings. Children, like most of us, accept their surroundings with little questioning until some aspect is brought to their attention. Buildings and building sites provide an opportunity for children to hone their observational skills and focus on structural phenomena they might otherwise pass by. Such settings are excellent places to conduct surveys and learn much about the process and content of science. Following are examples of some of the structural features of buildings that children can survey (see Illustration A4). [**Note:** Building sites can be dangerous places. Children should not visit them unaccompanied. All the work suggested here can be done by observation off site, i.e., from a safe distance or as a passer-by.]

• *Foundations.* All buildings have foundations. Most modern ones have concrete and brick foundations, but some older houses are set on stone pillars and large wooden beams. Students can seek out examples of all these in the area.

• *Walls and sides.* Most houses now are frame built; students can look for ongoing construction where the frame is still visible. They can record the pattern of the structure. They can observe how triangulation is used to provide strong shapes; using strips of stiff cardboard and brass paper fasteners to represent the shapes they see, they can test these shapes.

• *Brick work.* In some houses there is brick work. Students can look at the patterns made by bricklaying. Giving them their technical names is helpful. For example: bricks placed on their long sides are called *stretchers;* those with the short side facing are called *headers;* the layers of bricks are called *courses.* Students can represent what they see by making sketches of the patterns of brick work in a residential or commercial area.

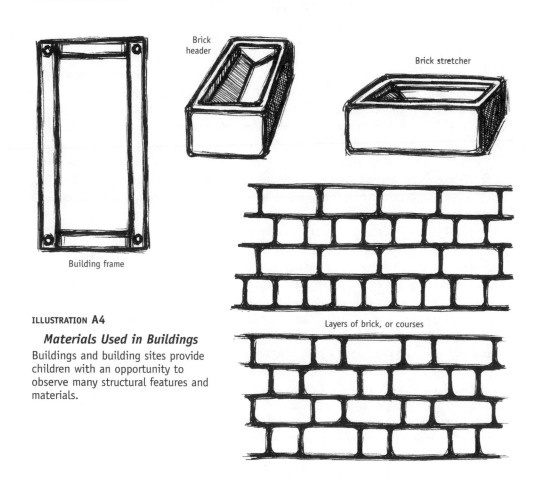

ILLUSTRATION A4

Materials Used in Buildings

Buildings and building sites provide children with an opportunity to observe many structural features and materials.

- *Roofs.* Most roofs have a covering of materials that are easy to put in place high on the sloping roof. Of course, they must be waterproof and easily kept in place. Students can make a survey of the roofing materials in the area. They can draw the patterns they see and observe how the ridge along the top of the roof is finished. Students can conduct a survey to answer such questions as: What are the most common coverings for roofs? What are the unusual ones? What different patterns do roof lines follow?

- *Paints and colors.* Students can make a survey of the colors used on the outside of local houses. They can develop a composite picture by investigating such questions as: What is the favorite color for window frames? Front doors? Balconies and porches? What colors are chosen most for painting the exterior walls of houses?

- *New materials.* Surveys can also highlight the variety of building materials used. For example, students might count and represent: How many houses have aluminum windows and doors? How many houses have plastic coverings on the window frames and doors? How many have a mixture of materials—brick, stone, wood—on their exterior?

Communicating and Displaying Information

The High/Scope Curriculum provides a means by which children's own chosen interests become activities that use their personal involvement to solve problems in the open manner of good science. The High/Scope *plan-do-review sequence* does more than merely unlock the gate to a successful way of working.

The "planning stage" provides an opportunity for teacher-child and child-child dialogue. This dialogue helps to shape the work, provides encouragement, and allows for guidelines and suggestions about procedures to be exchanged. It also creates a "public" awareness of what is going on. Dialogue in the planning stage begins the chain of events bound up in communication. It establishes that there are others interested in the questions addressed, how they will be investigated, and what the outcomes may be. It gives communicating the results a worthwhile and genuine purpose.

The "do" stage provides the power, the heightened interest, and the energy for the next stage as communication expands the ideas and activities engaged in by the students. Development during the doing phase sets the stage for the reviewing part of the sequence, when a description of the activities and their outcomes will be communicated. With something real to communicate—a description of a process, an accounting of what was learned—and a real and enthusiastic audience, the impetus to use effective means of communication is increased and the desire to do it well becomes a very important motivating force.

The "review" stage helps students to consolidate the knowledge they have gained and sets the stage for further activity. In recounting their experiences and observations, students are encouraged to organize their thoughts and convey to others what was meaningful about their activities. Because the reviewing stage is typically shorter than the doing stage, students must find ways to effectively summarize what they have done. Reviewing also helps students reflect on their experiences and consider what to do next. Are there still unanswered questions? Did the experiments suggest related avenues to explore? How can we communicate both the excitement of what we have learned and our enthusiasm for continuing the investigation?

Dialogue—verbally sharing procedures and results—is an important means of communication in science. Often overlooked, however, is the role that visually displaying results can play in communicating the scientific process and students' discoveries. In the rest of this section, options will be discussed for using visual display as the vehicle for communication in science. Just as it is important for all children to share their work verbally, so too it is important to provide opportunities for all children to display their work and to view the work of others. The emphasis should not be on adult-made polished displays that reflect the work of the teacher or a few selected students. Rather, displays should reflect the real work of all students as they grapple with issues of interest to them and create a picture of how the world functions.

Considerations of Space

Classroom facilities vary greatly, from cramped to spacious. School opportunities for displays are equally varied, from confinement to classrooms, or spaces in corridors, to larger scale opportunities in halls and open areas. The importance of the visual aspects of communication is often underestimated, especially in the cramped class-room. It is indisputable, though, that a great deal of what we learn is through the evidence of our eyes, rather than through our ears or other sensory organs alone. Quite apart from being informed, children (and adults) are excited, stimulated, and enriched by what they see. Material displayed should perform at least one of the three essential functions of display: to enhance the appearance of the area; to interest and inform some or all of the children; and to give the satisfaction of a real contribution to those involved in the work displayed.

Some teachers like to have two areas for display, one for finished work and one for work in progress. The first area can be used to showcase work that has run its course and reached a conclusion; it can present both the processes and the outcomes of the students' scientific investigations. The second area is where review-time work can be on temporary display, where half-finished charts can be pinned up for discussion; and where apparatus can be commented on. This display can create a sense of excitement as the changes each day reflect the ongoing discovery process. The finished space needs to be as large as can be afforded for science; the in-progress space can be smaller and might even rotate depending upon the area of the room where the work is being carried out. It is also a good idea to have a storage bin near the area where ongoing work can be safely and neatly looked after. Disorderly storage and general clutter in a room makes it difficult to focus on and observe the ongoing work; it also limits work efficiency. Although in a lively classroom, disorder is often present and can be a positive sign of active engagement, it is also one that should be managed. Cleanup time can take on added significance in this situation, as students determine how to maintain organization while at the same time permitting activity-based pursuits to continue.

Wall Displays

Whatever else a classroom lacks in terms of space, it will have walls, and these will afford a principal means of display. A trestle table, for example, can be erected when needed and placed against the wall. If space permits, one or more permanent tables for use in conjunction with wall displays are useful. Storage bins can be placed underneath the table(s) to conserve space (see Illustration A5 on pg. 126).

Pictorial work, charts and graphs, photographs, and diagrams all need mounting to create effective displays. A stock of old picture frames, without glass, is a quick and effective method for highlighting and giving a finished look to work without having to go to the trouble of cutting mounts. Double-sided cellophane tape will also hold work in place on wall displays. Finally, *good communication needs good labeling to carry its message.* Children can make these labels using a variety of techniques. For example, stencils, appliquéd letters, cutouts from magazines and newspapers, bold script, and varied fonts created on the computer—all are effective alternatives for creating eye-catching and informative labels.

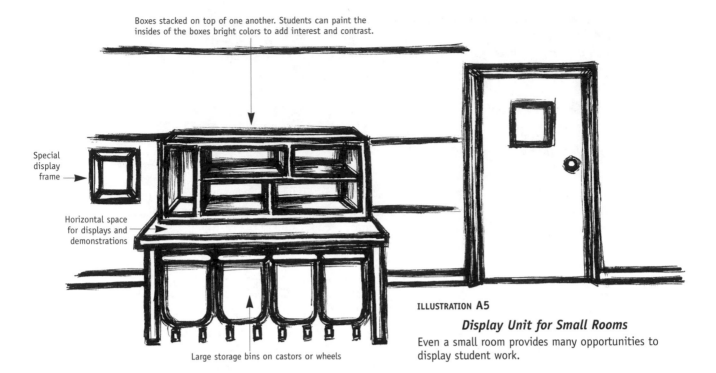

Boxes stacked on top of one another. Students can paint the insides of the boxes bright colors to add interest and contrast.

Special display frame →

Horizontal space for displays and demonstrations →

Large storage bins on castors or wheels

ILLUSTRATION A5

Display Unit for Small Rooms

Even a small room provides many opportunities to display student work.

Concertina Display Units

When wall space for display is limited, concertina (hinged and folded) display units can be made to increase the available surface area in the classroom. This method of display can also be used during special events, such as for parents and friends or children from other classes when extra display space is needed. Simply fix thick cardboard or hardboard sheets together so that they fold at the joins. Use wide packing tape to join the sheets, being sure to leave a gap between each sheet slightly wider than the material is thick. This allows for easy folding. The joints should be taped back and front. Smaller versions of this design can be made for tabletop displays. Make three or four sets of different sizes, for example, double- and triple-folded units. (See Illustration A6.)

Concertina units made from thick cardboard or from thin plywood or hardboard

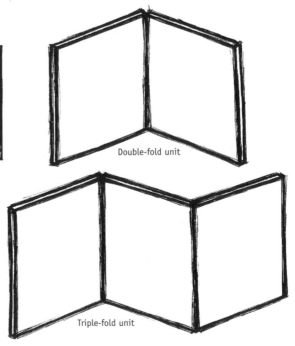

Double-fold unit

Triple-fold unit

ILLUSTRATION A6

Displays

Concertina display units can increase the available surface area in the classroom. Smaller versions of this design, such as small double- and triple-folded units, can be made for tabletop displays.

Temporary Display Units: Brick and Board Shelves and Cubes

Sometimes an urgent need for additional shelf space occurs, especially if many children have to store their work temporarily at the same time. To accommodate this need at the end of a work session, shelves can be rapidly built on bricks or blocks, using planks (see Illustration A7). Do not try to support planks longer than 3 feet without extra bricks or blocks at 2-foot intervals. Once this arrangement has served its purpose, planks and blocks can be stacked away until they are needed again.

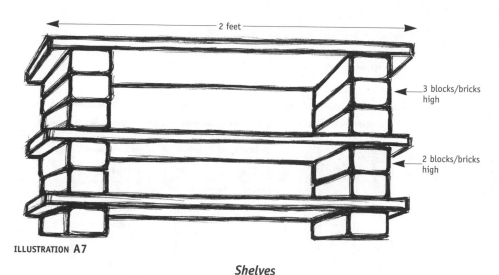

← 2 feet →

3 blocks/bricks
high

2 blocks/bricks
high

ILLUSTRATION **A7**

Shelves

Shelves can be rapidly constructed of boards supported by bricks or blocks. The space between shelves can be adjusted to accommodate the height of the objects displayed.

Other temporary display structures may be created. A shallow drawer painted white and with the handles removed makes a good display case for small collections. Adding a layer of sand, shells, pebbles, bones, or cones at the bottom can provide an effective background and emphasize the purpose behind the collection displayed on the surface. If you have a supply of cubical cardboard or plastic boxes about 12" by 15", these also make attractive display and storage units (see Illustration A8). They can be stacked and painted or covered with bright colors, both inside and out, to catch the eye.

ILLUSTRATION **A8**

Display Cubes

In addition to displaying objects inside the cubes, the way the cubes are piled up presents a design in itself.

Arranging the Display Space

Highlighting the work. Black mounts are effective for most written work (such as graphs and charts) because the light-color paper of the work shows up well against the dark background. Help children cut out their work and design the display; encourage them to leave ample space and avoid overcrowding. A few simple messages are often more telling than detailed explanations, which may be hard to see and read. Leave space for labels and other notes. A few arrows sometimes give a sense of direction. Before attaching the parts of the display, try laying everything out first to see how they fit. Make any necessary adjustments before completing the mounting. Fix the items with a touch of adhesive at each corner; pasting may cause wrinkles and problems in placing wet paper on the mounting sheet. Let the children design the sheet to tell its own story and reflect what they have done (see Illustration A9).

ILLUSTRATION **A9**

A Mounted Display Unit

Mounting the work on a background of contrasting color helps to highlight a display. Avoid overcrowding and keep labels and messages simple. Lay out everything to see how it fits before attaching the parts of the display.

Using multiple display strategies. A small display around the work of a single group is well-contained in ordinary classroom situations. However, when there is a considerable amount of material from a whole class, perhaps work distributed over several class periods, the problem is a different one. Not only will there be a great deal of material, but it may be of different kinds—some visual, some three dimensional, and some collections of objects.

Solving the problem of making the most of a limited classroom space for a large amount of material—or a major exhibition of science work—needs a plan. In planning, avoid putting all the material around the classroom walls. Try to arrange one display area that preserves the connections and continuity of the display. For example, this area could start in a corner of the room where the two walls provide a natural background for the display space. You can then clear an area in front of the walls to put up tables and screens, attracting attention to the display as a focal point in the room (see Illustration A10 on pg. 129).

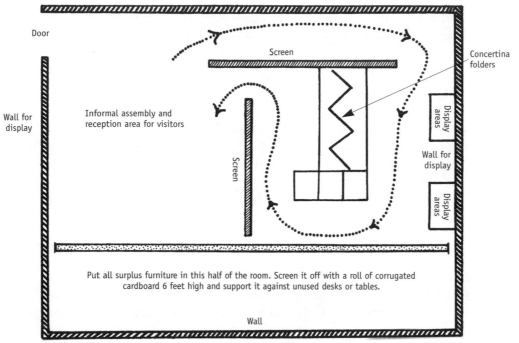

Wall

Door

Wall for display

Screen

Concertina folders

Informal assembly and reception area for visitors

Display areas

Wall for display

Screen

Display areas

Put all surplus furniture in this half of the room. Screen it off with a roll of corrugated cardboard 6 feet high and support it against unused desks or tables.

Wall

ILLUSTRATION A10

Using the Classroom as an Exhibition Space

In displaying a large amount of work, avoid putting all the materials around the classroom walls. Group the materials in areas to preserve their connections and to provide the display with continuity.

Student Involvement in Creating Displays

As much as possible, always include children in planning and arranging communications and displays. They will gain on many fronts: thinking about how to represent their work; exercising their visual judgment; reflecting on the lessons they learned and how to communicate them; and feeling a sense of worth as they see the display taking shape. If the teacher takes time and trouble to create opportunities for displaying student work, the children will themselves develop an appreciation for the importance of their scientific endeavors.

Part 2

Materials and Equipment

The teacher will inevitably be a partner in the classroom in the action—as well as in the dialogue. Teachers are called upon to provide practical assistance with manipulative tasks and sometimes to help complete over-ambitious construction activities. It will be important to have on hand a few simple tools and to become proficient at using them. A very firm table or small workbench will make a great difference both to the ease of working and to competence and confidence in doing jobs. It will assist greatly if the basic materials and tools listed at the end of this section are readily available.

Think "Simple"

In many people's minds, science work is thought of in terms of test tubes, special equipment, and complicated electronics. This apparently specialized apparatus, however, need not be present in the elementary school. In fact, many of the world's great discoveries were made with apparatus based on everyday materials and on observations of commonplace phenomena. Nowhere is this more important than in early education. With young children, we need to expose the underlying science with minimal dependence on equipment. For children, science activities often lead to great discoveries, for they are first-time experiences for them. This "first-timeness" liberates an enthusiasm in children, a sense of wonder that becomes the spur for further activity and concentrated effort. Much of this excitement can be lost by a pedantic insistence upon the "right" things being used.

An Example

A good example of the advantages of simplicity is in the use of comparative measurements. For the youngest children, lengths of string are just as good as tape measures for assessing differences; they will be concerned only with which is longest or shortest, rather than with absolute dimensions (see Illustration A11). It will be at a later stage when they want to know exactly how much longer or shorter that measurement needs to be in more conventional terms. In the former case, the children using the string need the excitement of quickly seeing the result, not the frustration of reading the tape measure to the nearest small unit—that comes later when arguments need to be decided on the basis of greater accuracy. At this stage, the strings show the results very clearly and are better than tape measures.

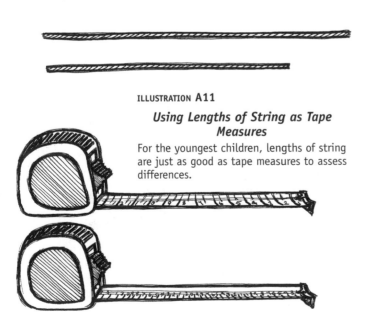

ILLUSTRATION **A11**

Using Lengths of String as Tape Measures

For the youngest children, lengths of string are just as good as tape measures to assess differences.

Begin With What Is Readily Available

In servicing practical activities, both children and teachers need to first ask: What is available? Next they can ask: How can I use these materials to help solve the problem? Often this act of thinking and improvising itself assists the problem-solving process, as it concentrates attention on essentials in the situation. Science is an empirical subject and is concerned with the practical, working out of ideas, especially at the primary school level. Here we are concerned more with starting points than end products. Thus, developing ideas about the use of simple materials may well open up student interest in a subject better than a formal introduction by the teacher. The creative manipulation of materials and the devising and setting up of experiments often opens the way for a realization of the need for more sophisticated apparatus. Again, children will come to look on materials as amenable to use in a variety of ways according to the needs of the situation. For instance, the common detergent bottle made of plastic can be a lighthouse in one context and a rain gauge in another (see Illustration A12).

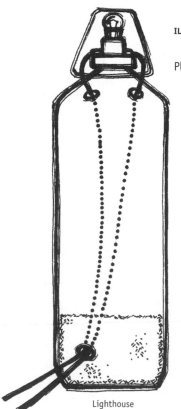

ILLUSTRATION A12

Uses for Plastic Detergent Bottles
Plastic bottles can be put to many uses in the study of science.

Lighthouse

Rain gauge

It can also be a musical instrument when peas or small nails are put inside as shakers. Sometimes work can be helped considerably by a few ready prepared items, which can overcome manipulative problems. A good example is the provision of ready-made electrical connection leads. These minimize the difficulties some children find in attaching wires to contacts. Crocodile clips at the ends of wires make excellent connectors and are easily made up by the teacher or a helper in advance of possible use (see Illustration A13).

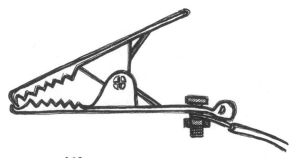

ILLUSTRATION A13

Crocodile Clip
Crocodile clips at the ends of wires make excellent connectors in the study of electricity.

Some supplies will need to be purchased, for substitutes are either hard to find or awkward to use. For example, one or two really powerful permanent magnets are essential, as is a varied collection of magnets children will collect. There are no substitutes either for a few, large, hand magnifiers. Again, children will collect smaller ones for themselves, and these will serve for some investigations. But for detailed observations, high-grade magnifiers are crucial if satisfactory results are to be obtained. The aim should always be to provide enabling materials and equipment that minimize the difficulties and keep the essentials of the problem clearly before the children.

Simple Tools for the Teacher's Use in Science

Below is a list of simple tools that teachers will want to have on hand. Their accessibility in the classroom allows students and teachers alike to improvise and to take advantage of spontaneous questions that arise in the course of scientific investigations.

- Hammer No. 0 or No. 1; Warrington type (not a heavy claw hammer)
- Brad awl size A $1\frac{1}{4}$". (This pierces holes by breaking the fibers; use before putting in screws.)
- 4" G clamp (or a clamp or vice)—this holds jobs firmly.
- 5" pincers
- Screwdrivers—large (10–12"); medium (4–6"); and small (2–3"); electrical, battery driven screwdrivers can also be handy for adult use.
- 5" universal pliers
- Junior hacksaw for cutting plastic and metal
- 8" tenon saw for cutting wood
- Wire stripper (bib stripper type)
- Hand drill with bits $\frac{1}{8}$", $\frac{3}{16}$", $\frac{1}{4}$" (not an electric drill)
- 6" triangular file
- Bench hook for cutting against
- Surform shaping tool (cuts wood, plastic, etc., like a file)
- Strong scissors

Equipment Generally Available in Schools and Classrooms

In addition to the tools that you will want to assemble, be aware of all the items you are likely to have available in the school and classroom that can be used for science activities. A list of commonly available equipment and materials follows:

- Writing paper—all kinds, including plain, lined, graph (squared), large for charts, drawing paper, colored papers
- Other paper—tracing paper, blotting paper, carbon paper, colored gummed back, tissue paper
- Paste—cold water, glue for general use, balsa cement
- Cardboard—thin for charts; thick and stiff for model making
- Scissors—round-ended safety scissors for younger children; pointed scissors for older children; one or two large pairs for cutting out shapes made of heavy materials

- Pins—large steel and large brass
- Thumbtacks—metal and metal covered in plastic
- Labels—glue-based and self-adhesive (including self-adhesive strips)
- Wall thermometer
- Cellophane tape—including wide, parcel-packaging tape
- Pencils, rulers, erasers
- String—different thicknesses, including twine and thread
- Clay—plasticine, modeling clay
- Paints—watercolors, either powdered or premixed
- Crayons—narrow for detail drawing and wide for labeling
- Paper clips—metal and plastic slip-on, brass fold-back eyelet type
- Rubber bands—assorted sizes (widths and lengths)
- Self-adhesive film—the type used for book covering
- Notebooks—spiral pads, memo pads
- Staplers—large and small
- Staple gun—tacker for teachers to use in mounting wall displays
- Hole punch—single, two-hole, and three-hole at standard widths
- Plastic containers—buckets and bowls
- Cleaning supplies—soap, detergent, towels

► *Part 3*
Measurement in Science

Measurement Techniques and Simple Devices

Timing and Timers and Time

While all classrooms need one or two "seconds" timers as part of their equipment, time measurement can also be done in broad terms, using other school-made devices. For example, some children will be conscious of the sunlight making its passage through different windows at different times of the day. What time is it? How long does it take? When does it seem to move fastest? These are all questions that can be answered with varying degrees of accuracy using child-made timing devices. The sun coming through the windows marks the passage of time in large intervals and may be a starting point for considering the passage of time in terms of the sun's movement.

Sundial (stick shadow). In an open space, have students set up a stick shadow and mark the shadow at regular intervals during a day, say, at 9, 10, 11, 12, 1, 2, and 3 o'clock. What happens to the length of the shadow? Students can make further observations at the set intervals and mark the length of the shadow on the ground. Place the times against the shadow marks (see Illustration A14).

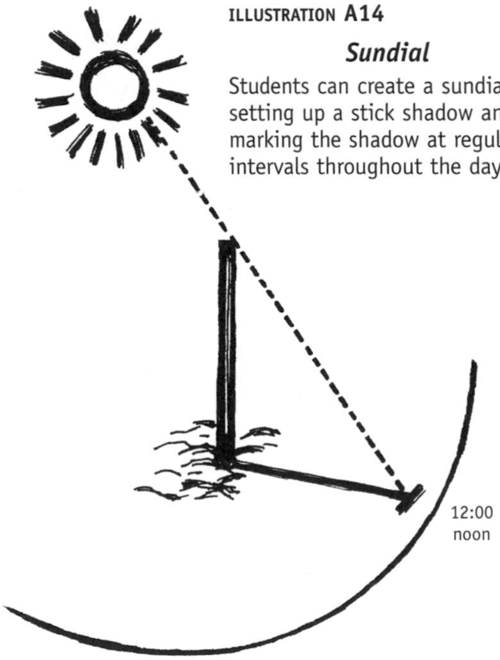

Pendulum. Timing school activities will often require devices that indicate shorter units of time. There are several possibilities for creating such devices. The simplest is the pendulum, which can be a very exact way to measure the passage of time. Children can make a pendulum consisting of a piece of thin string with a small weight on the end. When put in a place where it can swing freely,

ILLUSTRATION A14

Sundial

Students can create a sundial by setting up a stick shadow and marking the shadow at regular intervals throughout the day.

12:00 noon

a pendulum can measure seconds quite well (see Illustration A15 on pg. 135). The total length of the pendulum should be exactly 39 inches (1 meter). The accuracy depends on the length, even $\frac{1}{8}$ inch longer or shorter makes a difference. Don't worry about the weight on the bottom or the width of the swing. It is the length that matters. Set up a pendulum and test it by answering these questions (use a timer or a watch or a clock with a second hand):

• When the length is exactly 39 inches, how many swings are there in a minute? (If the length is right, it will be 60.)

• Shorten the string by one inch. How many swings now?

• Lengthen the string by one inch to make it 40 inches. How many swings to the minute?

• Get the length back to exactly 39 inches and retime the pendulum. Let it have a big swing. Does it still do 60 swings to the minute? Let it have a short swing. How many now to the minute?

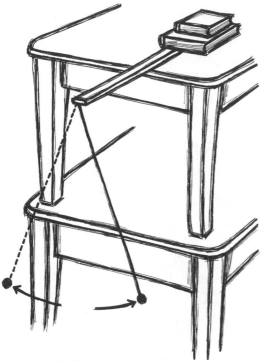

ILLUSTRATION **A15**

Constructing a Pendulum

Children can create a simple pendulum by attaching a piece of thin string with a weight attached to the end of a ruler.

Sand clocks. Sometimes a measurement device in-between the slow speed of the shadow stick and the fast speed of the pendulum is required. Students can make a sand clock and calibrate it. The secret of success with a sand clock is to have very fine, very dry sand. If none is available, the students can dry and sieve coarse sand for use through a nylon stocking sieve. Students can make a more accurate sand clock from two bottles as below. Use clear plastic bottles to avoid the danger of breakage (see Illustration A16).

Get two identical clear plastic bottles. Fill one bottle halfway with clean, fine dry sand. Cut a ring of cardboard to be an exact fit over the bottle tops without extending over the outside edges. Make a small, clean (clear) hole in the center of the cardboard. Put the cardboard on top of the bottle with sand in and the second bottle above. Have one student hold the bottles tightly together while another student fixes adhesive tape to keep them together. Invert the bottles and the sand will run from one to the other. Stick a paper scale on the outside of one bottle, then calibrate it using a watch as a timer. This will make a good timer. Students can experiment to get the size of the hole in the cardboard right.

ILLUSTRATION **A16**

Making Sand Clocks

To make a successful sand clock, sieve coarse sand through a nylon stocking funnel into a clear plastic bottle. Students can make a more accurate sand clock by using two plastic bottles.

Sieve

Nylon funnel

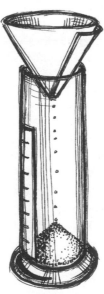

Plastic bottle

Water clocks. Water clocks have been used since ancient times. Some were very elaborate, while others were quite simple. The problem is to get a small-enough flow of water so that the clock works for a long-enough period without needing refilling. Below is a water clock that is easy for students to make. Get a plastic detergent container with a screw cap over a fine nozzle. Also, get a second, clear container for the first one to rest on; it could be a clear plastic bottle with the top cut off. This second container must hold more liquid than the first container. Cut off the bottom of the detergent (first) container. Plug the normal outlet hole with clay or plasticine. Make a very small hole (a pinhole) for the water to come out into the clear container. Calibrate the clear container with a paper strip (see Illustration A17).

Remove the screw-on stopper, leaving the exit hole and its parts intact and filling the shaped part with a plug of plasticine. As near the center as possible, make a very small hole for as little water as possible to flow out. The normal larger hole will make the clock "run out" of time too quickly.

Stand the water clock against a wall or another source of support when operating it; it will easily fall unless the base of the long container is weighted with plasticine.

Have students try variations on this design and solve these problems:

• What happens if you just use the original hole?

• What is the effect of larger holes? Smaller holes?

• Can you invent a clock with different rates of flow for different timings?

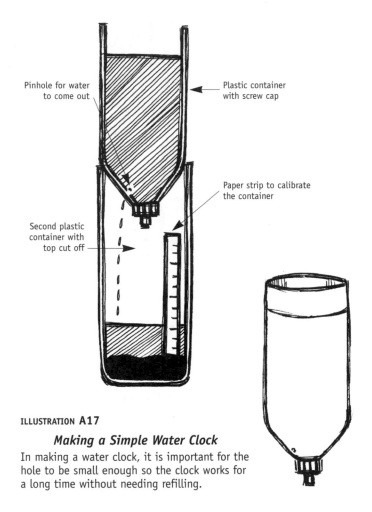

ILLUSTRATION A17

Making a Simple Water Clock

In making a water clock, it is important for the hole to be small enough so the clock works for a long time without needing refilling.

Weighing Devices

Weighing light objects. Quite often, simple weighing devices are needed. Children can easily improvise these items of equipment, especially when the measurements required are in terms of comparisons, not actual standard units.

For example, students can make yardstick balances with holes at each end for attaching pans or objects for weighing. Use a paper clip slide to trim the balance to the horizontal. Stretched springs or elastic bands also make useful weighing devices, and they can easily be calibrated against standard weights if required, although the accuracy needs regular checking as the elastic stretches with use. Students can use different thicknesses of elastic to make balances for different ranges. The elastic bands are easily purchased at sewing supply stores; students may also be able to bring in elastic scraps from sewing projects at home. (See Illustration A18 on pg. 137.)

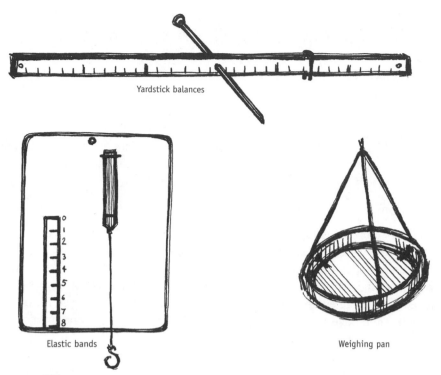

Yardstick balances

Elastic bands

Weighing pan

ILLUSTRATION A18

Weighing Devices

Simple weighing devices can be improvised when measurements are made for purposes of comparison and do not need to be in standard units.

Weighing heavy objects. Sometimes heavier and more awkward objects need to be weighed. Students can make a simple device from an old upholstery spring and two tin cans. First, get a medium-sized coil-type upholstery spring. Students can use various sizes of springs in this design, such as those obtained from chairs, car seats, and old mattresses. Then have students get a tin, with a top cut off cleanly (no sharp edges), into which the spring will fit entirely. Finally, have them find a smaller tin that will fit into the larger tin. Again the top should be cut off cleanly, and the edges of both tins should be smoothed with a file. The calibration can be made by covering the inner tin with paper or painting on the markings (see Illustration A19). This balance is not very good for small weights, but it will weigh liquids and heavier items. The students can calibrate it by using known standard weights.

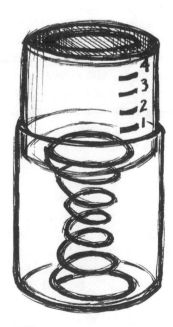

ILLUSTRATION A19

Upholstery Spring

Students can make a simple weighing device from an old upholstery spring and two tin cans. The device can be calibrated by covering the inner tin with paper or painting on the markings.

The Metric System:
Communication in the Standard Measure of Science

The Improvised Conversion of Equipment to Metric Measures

With scientists universally using metric measures, schools will need to consider the wisdom of making some metric measures for themselves. This is an especially urgent need when working with younger children because they are still forming their concept of the real significance of measures. Some suggestions are given below for the improvisation of metric measures—first, to make equipment available quickly; and second, to provide schools with uses for existing material.

Metric Weights

A simple method for adjusting 2-lb. and 1-lb. weights from avoirdupois to metric units is to put the weight to be adjusted into a suitably sized cardboard box with a lid. Have students seal the lid on tightly with cellophane tape and pierce a hole in the corner of the box. They should then add fine dry sand until enough weight has been added to produce either 1 kilogram (for the 2-lb. weight) or 500 grams (for the 1-lb. weight). Then have students seal the small filler hole with tape and mark the appropriate weight on the box.

Where a reduction in weight is required (for example, when converting 8 ozs. to 200 grams; 4 ozs. to 100 grams; or ½ oz. to 10 grams), a different procedure is recommended before the weight is put in the box and treated as above. If it is a ring type of weight, the teacher or an older student can cut the metal ring through with a junior hacksaw, and this will probably make a reduction of weight below the quantity required. Box the weight and treat it as before (adding sand) to adjust the weight suitably. If the smaller weight is of a solid rather than a ring type, then cut a "V" shaped piece of metal from it with the junior hacksaw; if necessary, enlarge the "V" until the weight is reduced below that required. Box the weight and treat it as before—adding sand and labeling the box appropriately. One of the virtues of this boxing system is that it obliterates entirely any markings on the old weight and creates the new one in a form that is easily convenient for remarking.

There are other similar procedures that students can use to adjust metal weights and convert them from avoirdupois to metric measures. Instead of sand, weight adjustments can be made by affixing clay or cement to the top of the weight. Where a weight needs to be reduced, the teacher or older student can drill a suitably sized hole to reduce the weight below the desired level and adjust accordingly by adding material into the hole until it is of the required weight. Whatever the method of adjustment used, it will be important to obliterate the old markings by taping over them or covering them in some way and then remarking them. Furthermore, it will be necessary to check the final product carefully against some standard metric weight as a control. It must be stressed that the improvised weights are of an approximate order only, and they should be checked on a finer measuring scale than those on which they will normally be used.

The following table indicates the approximate adjustment that can be made to common avoirdupois measures to transform them into useful metric alternatives:

2 lbs.	plus	approximately 93 grams converts to 1 kilogram
1 lb.	plus	approximately 46 grams converts to 500 grams
8 ozs.	minus	26 grams converts to 200 grams
4 ozs.	minus	13 grams converts to 100 grams
½ oz.	minus	4 grams converts to 10 grams

Scales and Spring Balances

Many domestic scales can be recalibrated by simply covering the old calibrations with plain paper and then remarking against standard weights. It is sometimes possible to simplify the number of calibrations and make the scale more useful for school purposes in this way. The larger type of parcel balances can easily be recalibrated by producing a new ring to stick over the existing one. Some may be available commercially, and these might be bought cheaply and recalibrated.

Most spring balances of the extension-type have a dual scale on them already. If this is so, it is easy for students to cover the avoirdupois side with either paper or tape. Spring balances that have only a single calibration in avoirdupois units can be converted quite easily with a plain scale affixed for calibration against standard metric weights.

Capacity Measures

Measures of capacity can be made from existing vessels. The following seem the most useful in conducting science activities:

- 2 pints will convert to a 1 liter measure by **adding** .054 liter

- 1 pint will convert to 500 milliliters by **adding** .017 liter

If a small measure is wanted (for example, a 10-milliliter measure), students will find that some bottle tops will serve excellently for this purpose. All these improvisations will call for a recalibration of the vessel. Students should use waterproof adhesive tape for this purpose. Semi-transparent plastic vessels can be marked by: (a) scratching a notch on the outside to the required height; (b) filling the vessel with a dark coloring material; and (c) marking the vessel evenly all round at the level of the liquid with waterproof ink.

Rulers

An easy method for recalibrating rulers is for students to apply ready-made calibrated tape to the ruler. One limitation of tape is its tendency to stretch, and it is very difficult to recalibrate longer measuring sticks without a considerable amount of "creep" on the tape. Tapes are likely to peel off if the rules are not well-cleaned before taping. Where longer rules are to be cut to a new length in metric units, students should cut them to a dead length, that is, without stop ends. This will make for a greater accuracy of use by the children, and it will be easier to affix tape or make fresh markings. If foot-long rulers are to be cut, they can be conveniently converted into one 20-centimeter length and one 10-centimeter length. These lengths will obviously have their uses. Yardsticks can also be used; however, there is a temptation to reduce them to 25 centimeter lengths, whereas most teachers feel it is far better for the child to get used to using measures that go up in even multiples of 10, that is, 10 centimeters, 20 centimeters, and so on. Emulsion paint is the most suitable for obliterating markings, as it is quick drying and covers well with one coat. However, incised markings will always show through. For the greatest permanency, students can cover the paint with a clear polyurethane varnish.

► *Part 4*
Testing and Analysis

Students can perform many simple tests and examine the properties of materials with simple procedures.

Constituent Mixtures

Sorting objects according to their attributes is an activity commonly undertaken in High/Scope classrooms. The physical analysis of mixtures of materials is a science activity that will extend this type of learning. Below are some examples of the kinds of constituent mixtures that students can explore.

Mixed Fruits

What types of different fruits make up the packages of mixed dried fruits commonly used in the kitchen? How many of each kind are in a package? Children must first identify the different fruits and put aside a specimen of each. Next, working in groups of three or four, children can start separating the different constituents. They can give them temporary identities for the purposes of the work, perhaps numbering or naming them arbitrarily. They can then answer questions such as the following: How many different types of fruit are there? How many fruits of each type are in the package? Are there equal numbers of each type in the mixture? What sort of fruit is most used in the mixture? What sort is used least? How do the fruits differ from each other in terms of size, color, shape, texture, taste, etc.? What are the real names for the fruits? Are the fruits whole or in parts? What parts of fruits are in the package (for example, there may be peel in some mixtures)?

The results can be set out both in chart or tabular form and as numerical statements. Examples of each of the identified fruits can be displayed together with its name, with pictures of the fruit in its natural state, and with information about its growth and nutrition.

Mixed Seeds

A procedure similar to that used for analyzing packages of mixed fruits can be applied to the packages of mixed seeds used to feed birds. An added benefit is that the analysis may require some additional investigation; while common seeds such as corn and sunflower seeds are in the mixture, teachers and students may find that less common seeds are also included (for example, thistle seed and various woodland plant seeds). Students may analyze a variety of mixtures. For example, mixed corn feed is relatively simple to separate and identify. Others mixtures may have more unusual elements. Students can generate the factors on which they want to compare the seeds in the mixture. In addition to obvious variables such as size, color, and shape, students may also notice other differences. For example, do the seeds have coverings? Are certain types of seeds more variable in appearance than others?

Mixed Candies

Packages of mixed candies are another obvious choice for this type of sorting activity. In addition to selling prepackaged mixtures, many stores offer bulk candy bins from which one can create a customized mixture of sweets. Students and teachers can choose their own combinations, deliberately varying the candies along a number of dimensions. As with the dried fruit, one attraction of this type of analysis is that you can eat the materials after you have compiled the results!

Ferrous Objects in a Room

How can all the ferrous (iron) objects in a room be found? First, children will need to experiment with magnets to establish that magnets only pick up, or stick to, ferrous materials. During this experimenting, children will be able to answer the following questions based on their experiences: Do magnets pick up anything without iron in them? Do magnets work through coverings such as paint? Paper? Plastic? Cloth? Other metals, such as brass or chrome plating?

To provide opportunities for all these investigations, teachers should have items and materials that exhibit all of the properties mentioned above. These items, which can be collected from everyday sources, include the following: iron hooks or screws covered with a thin layer of brass; solid brass hardware; plastic-covered curtain wire; uncovered curtain wire; metal strips covered with paper; metal strips covered with cloth; and pieces of cloth, pieces of wood, cardboard, paper, and plastic. There should also be painted iron items, aluminum pieces and copper wire, and metal and plastic paper clips.

When children have established to their own satisfaction the power of the magnet to detect ferrous items, they can begin examining any objects in the room that they suspect are ferrous. Children can work as individuals or in small groups. To record their results, children could make a plan of the room (or several plans, one for each area of the room) and label the different objects they test. They can also record their results on various charts and tables that they devise.

The Strength of Different Shapes

How strong are different shapes of building materials made from single strips of paper? Students can set up a testing bridge situation, as illustrated below. Make beams of different shapes (round, triangular) with rolled or folded paper, rest the beams on brick piers at either end, and place small boxes containing various weights of nails on the beams to test their strength (see Illustration A20).

Round beams. Have students cut three strips of paper, each 11" × 2", and roll each strip round a pencil to form a tube. This tube is the "beam" to be tested. Use cellophane tape about two inches from each end to retain the shape of the tube. Take the pencil out of the paper tube. Use two bricks at either end as piers, placed 4" apart, and place the three beams parallel to one another and ½" apart across the piers. Fill a small box or boxes with increasing numbers of nails to see how much weight the beams can support. Record the results. Next, have students place the piers 2" apart. Test this arrangement with loads of nails and have the students record the results. What effect does the spacing between the piers have on the ability of the beams to support the weight of the nails?

Triangular beams. Take three strips of paper cut to the same size as above (11" × 2") and fold each lengthwise into four equal parts. Open out the folded strip and refold it to make a triangular shape (see Illustration A20 on pg. 142). Keep the shape in place with narrow cellophane tape strips 2" from each end. This now makes a triangular beam to test. Place the three beams ½" apart on the test piers, set 4" apart, and test the strength of the beams as before; repeat this procedure with the supporting piers 2" apart and record the results. Have students compare the four test results in which the shape of the beam and the distance between the supporting piers have been varied. Which arrangement is the strongest? Which is the weakest?

Extensions. Students can extend the experiments by increasing and decreasing the distances between the two supporting piers. They can also try other beam shapes, such as flat strips or squared beams. Another variation would be to try different thicknesses of paper for the beam shapes.

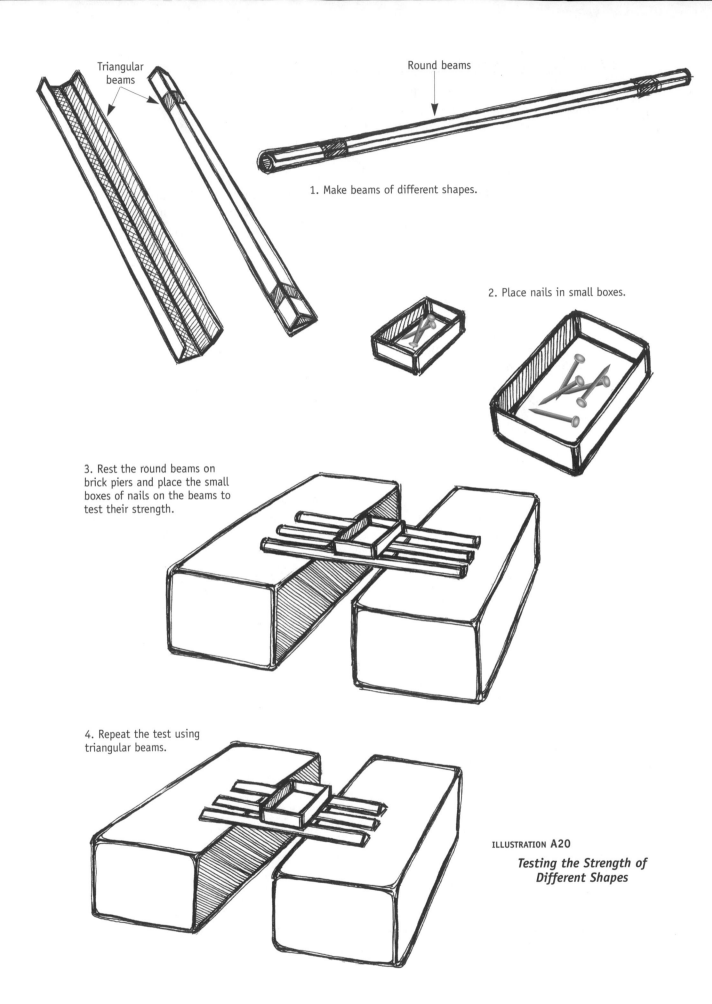

Triangular beams

Round beams

1. Make beams of different shapes.

2. Place nails in small boxes.

3. Rest the round beams on brick piers and place the small boxes of nails on the beams to test their strength.

4. Repeat the test using triangular beams.

ILLUSTRATION A20

Testing the Strength of Different Shapes

ENERGY AND CHANGE

Waterproof Properties of Different Materials

Waterproof quality is an important feature of many materials, especially when used for clothing and shelter. Testing materials can be an interesting activity for children who have already observed how their own clothes have either become wet or have resisted the rain.

Collect various materials of approximately the same thickness. Include, for example, cotton, nylon, wool, plastic sheeting, paper, and leather. Cut 4" (10 cm) squares of each material for testing. Place the test pieces on a large sheet of white blotting paper or other fairly absorbent paper. Make a colored solution with diluted ink, food coloring, or water soluble dye. Using a dropper (a pen filler, an eye dropper, a dropper bottle, or a drop falling from a paintbrush), have students put 10 drops of the color solution on each piece to be tested (see Illustration A21). Allow a set time, for example 3 to 5 minutes, to elapse. Then have the students make the following inspections:

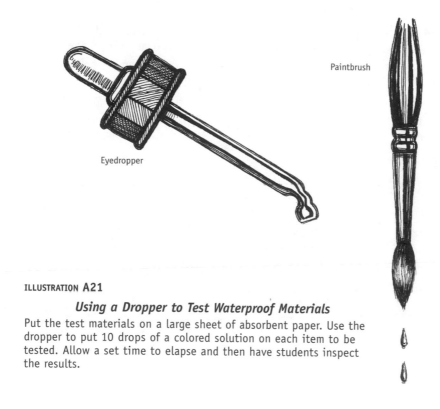

Paintbrush

Eyedropper

ILLUSTRATION **A21**

Using a Dropper to Test Waterproof Materials
Put the test materials on a large sheet of absorbent paper. Use the dropper to put 10 drops of a colored solution on each item to be tested. Allow a set time to elapse and then have students inspect the results.

• Inspect the blotting paper to see any markings left by the water soaking through the material. Have students note the evidence using a scale; for example: 0 = no penetration; 1 = some penetration; 2 = much penetration. Older students may develop a more elaborate scale.

• Inspect the material itself to see over what area the water had been absorbed. Have students note the evidence on a scale similar to the one(s) they devised above.

• Feel the material to see how wet the marked areas feel. Have students note the evidence on the scale; for example: 0 = not wet; 1 = wet only on the surface; 2 = damp throughout; 3 = wet throughout. Again students can devise their own scales for observing and recording the results.

As another way of representing the results, have students place the materials tested in their order of water resistance (from least to most, or vice versa). Have them discuss which material would be best for a raincoat. Which would let the most wet through? Are there times when you want a material to not be water resistant? What materials would serve those purposes?

Students can also investigate the reverse process of drying. Have them soak all the specimens that retain water and then hang them up on a line to dry in the same order as their waterproofness. At regular intervals, students can check the materials for dryness and record the results. Students can test for dryness using several criteria:

- Feel—Test the materials by gently rubbing them on the hand or cheek.

- Appearance—Do the materials look dry? Are they dry on just one side or on both sides?

- Smear test—Do the materials leave a moist smear when rubbed on a window?

After the results are recorded, have students place the specimens in order of speed of drying. How does this order compare to the order of waterproofness? Which materials would be most suitable for a coat? Are there situations where you would *not* want something to dry quickly? Which materials would be suitable for those purposes?

The question of how to waterproof material is a good extension of this investigation. For example, pose the question: How could you waterproof cotton cloth? Provide a supply of 4" (10 cm) squares of cotton cloth; you can cut up old shirts or handkerchiefs for this activity. (**Note:** Nylon fabric or synthetic materials generally are not useful for these experiments.) Through a dialogue approach with the children, have them examine and discuss the waterproofing properties of different coatings, such as oil, wax, fat, paint, and plastic stuck to the fabric. Display the results in chart form.

Seeds and Water

Mung bean seeds germinate quickly and are good for investigating the sprouting and growth of seeds. The seeds are inexpensive and are easily obtained through seed catalogs and garden stores. Local produce sellers may also help you locate packages of seeds. Here are some questions the students can consider:

- Will the seeds germinate on their own if one or two are left in the package?

- When are seeds usually planted outdoors? Why? Would seeds germinate more rapidly near the central heating system? What would happen to seeds put into the refrigerator?

- Do seeds need warmth only? Do seeds need moisture to germinate? Will they grow under water?

- Do seeds planted in soil all grow at the same rate?

- Is there a right way up to plant seeds? What happens if some are planted one way up and others the reverse way?

(**Note:** Try these experiments with large seeds such as broad beans as well as the smaller mung beans.)

Have students set up experiments with the seeds set in various ways: on moist cloth, on dry cloth, left on an open saucer; in moist soil, in dry soil, left on an open saucer; and in moist sand, in dry sand, left on an open saucer

Students can either work individually or in groups to carry out these experiments. See that the conditions are well-controlled, so that the dry soil and sand is really dry, and the moist soil is kept moist with exactly the same amount of water in each sample. In the case of the soil and the sand, see that the seeds are set at the same depths. Put the groups of experiments in a place where they will get the same amount of light and not be disturbed, but can be observed easily by the students. The results can be communicated in a variety of ways, through charts, diagrams, tape recordings of procedures, and a display of actual specimens.

If an interest in seeds develops among the children, there are several longer term experiments they can set up. It is worth remembering that in school, longer term science studies can go on in parallel with shorter term interests and activities. Here are some activities to try to answer students' questions about where plants come from and under what conditions they grow:

• Have students bring into the classroom a shovel full of top soil from any part of the area that apparently has no plants growing on it. Set this soil in a dish, keep it warm and moist, and see if anything grows.

• After a walk on open ground where the natural vegetation grows thickly, have students collect all the mud from their shoes. Put the mud in a dish, keep it warm and moist, and see if anything grows.

• If the school has an open site with garden space around it, have students clear and dig over a square yard of ground until it appears cleared of plants. Have them observe what happens as time goes on and record the results.

► *Part 5*
Safety and Science

The study of science is exciting, but it also holds potential hazards for students as well as for any wildlife that students may be examining. Below are some basic procedures and criteria to follow to ensure that science education at the elementary level is carried out safely.

Adult Supervision

It should be assumed that anything done in school, even with adult supervision, may be attempted out of school without any adult available. Adults should inform children of these potential risks and explain the dangers. It is also helpful for teachers to inform parents about the kinds of science activities being conducted in the classroom. This will not only help parents anticipate some of the activities that children might want to try on their own, but will also give them the opportunity to become involved and supervise their children as they investigate and extend their learning at home.

Sources of Heat

Sources of heat should be limited to the following:

- Hot air from a heating system in the classroom

- Heat from a conventional domestic radiator

- Warm water from a temperature-controlled tap (not from an electric kettle)

- Heat from the sun

Note that the above list precludes the use of the following:

- Open flames of any kind

- Electrical heaters and fans

- Gas burners and spirit lamps

Electrical Energy

Electrical energy should always be from battery powered sources. Electricity from a main electrical outlet should NOT be used in any work, even via a low-voltage supply. Where essential equipment such as computers are connected to main outlets, the plugs should be of a safeguarded pattern and never handled by the children. Where rechargeable cells are used, the charging process should be done privately by the teacher in the absence of the pupils. Plugging in batteries to charge them is not a task for children at school.

Tools

When tools are used in school they should be restricted to simple, nonpower ones, such as hammers, pincers, pliers, hand-operated screwdrivers (not battery driven for this age group), bradawls, gimlets. Drills are best avoided, and where possible predrilled materials should be available. When construction work is undertaken it should always be on a firm surface. If cutting is essential the materials cut should be of a "soft wood" or hardboard and cut with a junior hacksaw. A vice or clamp to hold material to be cut is essential. Cutting of hand-held material should be prohibited. Knives are not suitable for children to use in these contexts. Suitable scissors should be available for cutting, round-tipped for younger children and pointed for older children. Whenever questions about safety arise, the best solution is for the teacher to supply partly prepared material, leaving the final construction decisions to the children by means within their safe capabilities.

Living Material

If living material is used, it should be handled sensitively. Plants should be carefully treated, and only common species should be removed for use in school. It is best to grow plants in school from wild plant seed or seeds purchased specifically for that purpose. Investigations involving molds and fungi and dead material generally are best avoided. The likelihood of infection is too great to overlook. When animals are kept, they should be held under as near-natural conditions as possible. In the case of mammals, it will usually be best for them to be temporary visitors to the classroom; the care of mammals in schools, other than laboratories, is not easy. Small animals such as ants, snails, worms, butterflies, and moths should be also be housed in conditions as near their natural habitats as possible. When their life in school is at an end, they should be returned to their natural surroundings and a teaching point should be made of this procedure.

Kitchen Foods and Chemicals

Keep in mind that not all the substances found in the kitchen are safe. Safe items include soap, salt, sugar, washing soda, food coloring, lemon juice, vinegar, flour, olive oil, and dried foods. Unsafe items include bleach, oven cleaner, mineral spirits, kerosene, metal polish, and ammonia. Safety in the kitchen also means that items handled and used for experimentation should not be eaten. Keep extra supplies of these edible materials on hand; make sure that children understand when their investigations involve *eating* the materials and when they entail *handling* the materials.

Environmental Safety

There are a few basic rules to observe concerning outdoor work. These rules are for the benefit of the children as well as for the wildlife they will be studying:

   • *Wear appropriate footwear.* Children's footwear should allow their feet to stay dry and should minimize the risks of slipping and falling.

   • *Do not work alone outdoors.* Children should always work in pairs or groups and not take off to observe or collect materials on their own. If the location involves waterside activities, this will be an especially important rule.

   • *Stay on the ground.* Tree climbing, rock climbing, and the like are not activities for school-inspired work for young children.

   • *Avoid handling animals.* Remember that animals are best observed, not handled. Handling often injures the animal, and sometimes the animal can injure the handler. When children are taken on farm visits, they need to be prepared well beforehand about how to approach animals.

   There is an increasing need to create an environmental awareness in children, one that includes a respect for all living things and the environment in which they live. Science education provides an opportunity for children to learn valuable lessons that will affect their attitudes and behavior for the rest of their lives.

The Development of Problem-Solving Skills

The Definition of Problem Solving

Problem solving is deliberate discovery making, or discovery by intent. A problem is a situation in which there are apparently more unknown elements than known elements. The solution depends on discovering how to either expose more known elements or deal directly with the unknown factors. The problem solver then reconstructs the balance of knowledge in the situation to favor the known over the unknown elements.

Problem Solving: The Way Into Science

Discovery methods are the basis of active learning in education, and this is certainly true in science. In fact, science education is all about problem solving. For students, successful problem solving is a liberating and motivating educational tool. For teachers to use these powerful forces, it helps to know something of the nature of problems and the process of problem solving.

Levels of Complexity in Problem Solving

The problem-solving process depends in part on the level of complexity of the problem. This process may be thought of as having four levels, listed below. In this hierarchical arrangement, levels II and III correspond to what most people accept as the definition of a problem. Level IV most closely resembles the disciplined and rigorous true scientific procedure.

  • *Level I: The intuitive response.* The solver immediately recognizes the nature of the problem and its solution.

  • *Level II: The procedural response.* The solver knows the rules or procedures for obtaining a solution.

  • *Level III: The improvisation or trial-and-error approach.* The solver knows neither the solution nor the rules for obtaining it, but must improvise procedures to create the rules and obtain a solution.

  • *Level IV: The methodological approach.* The solver has to reformulate the problem to make it manageable, to make the question answerable. Having reformulated it, the solver tests the validity of the new definition. Then the solver improvises rules and procedures to produce a solution.

It is important for teachers to understand and appreciate these levels so that they may better recognize where children, and they themselves, stand in relation to this process. Within each classroom, students' problem-solving operations will be at differing levels of complexity; the same student may operate at different levels in different contexts. At the primary grade level, most children will be at levels I and II; few, if any, will be at level III. By contrast, the complexity of academic and interpersonal problems that teachers deal with most of the time means that they are typically operating at levels III and IV.

Stages in the Problem-Solving Process

There are many types of problems and many possible models for solving them. To make this process comprehensible and workable for teachers, the process of solving a problem is divided into six identifiable stages:

  • *Stage 1.* The solver recognizes that there is a problem with some element(s) that can be identified and labeled.

• *Stage 2.* The definable element(s) are examined. Other information is collected (for example, from memory, records, past experiences, observation of the environment, etc.). The information is placed in context and related to the parameters of the problem.

• *Stage 3.* The total information now available is analyzed and structured into possible plans for the solution(s).

• *Stage 4.* The plan considered most promising as a solution is selected from the possibilities for trial.

• *Stage 5.* The selected plan is used to address the problem.

• *Stage 6.* The effectiveness of the plan is assessed. If a satisfactory solution is achieved, the problem is regarded as having been resolved. If not, another one of the solutions is tried and/or the problem is further redefined and the cycle is repeated.

Qualities Required of the Problem Solver

The steps involved in problem solving are only one aspect of this complicated process. Equally important is the human dimension. In order to succeed in this process of problem solving, an individual needs to possess a variety of capacities. The problem solver should be able to:

• Perceive that a problem exists and be able to define it sufficiently and clearly so that it retains its essential characteristics

• Accept that he/she wants to and can solve the problem

• Bring to mind relevant information (concepts, experiences, observations), using memory and data-gathering skills, and assess whether the current information is sufficient for a solution

• Search actively for additional relevant information that may be useful in enlarging the knowledge base available in seeking a solution

• Establish links between components of the knowledge base (concepts, materials, facts) and the problem formulated so that the knowledge can be applied toward finding a solution

• Be brave enough to take a risk with a solution and face failure

• Be able to adopt a feasible and creative, but clear-sighted, approach to generating new solutions when previous attempts fail

• Make decisions based on the most likely solution and carry through in implementing them

• Overcome failure when a selected solution proves unsuccessful

• Monitor, criticize, and revise solutions and methods of attacking a problem

• Add new information to the store of rules when a preferred solution is successful or an improvement is effective

• Develop an increasing ability to work through processes carefully and systematically

• Make continuous attempts to match effort to initial goals, particularly in the face of negative results

• Possess these qualities, or show evidence of being able to develop them: curiosity and an inquiring mind; persistence and perseverance; and flexibility

• Begin to develop these mature attributes: independence of thinking; open-mindedness; and confidence when handling new and unknown ideas and situations

Index

W

About the Author

<small>Distinguished British author and educator</small>

Frank F. Blackwell

has contributed to science education in a wide range of professional roles. Having earned an M.A. degree in Curriculum Studies, Blackwell began his career as a classroom teacher and headmaster at the early childhood, primary, and secondary levels. He became involved in the development of children's science curricula during the 1960s as a Nuffield Foundation Research Fellow in Science Education, serving on the team that developed the Nuffield Junior Science Project series. His contributions to science education extend to radio and television, where he has served as a scriptwriter, consultant, and researcher for science programming. For some 12 years, he was an Inspector of Schools in the London area. During this time, he also served as a university lecturer in teacher education and was seconded as director of a five-year national project in developing the use of new technologies in education in the early years. Blackwell then moved to the Netherlands to assume the post of Chief of Division with the Bernard Van Leer Foundation. After five years in this post he became Senior Advisor to the President of the High/Scope Educational Research Foundation. In addition to authoring this Elementary Science Activity Series, Blackwell is co-author of another High/Scope Press publication, *Elementary Curriculum: Science*, as well as Series Consultant for all the Elementary Curriculum Guides published by High/Scope Press.